PHONICS
in
PROPER PERSPECTIVE

ARTHUR W. HEILMAN
The Pennsylvania State University

D1041037

CHARLES E. MERRILL BOOKS, INC. • COLUMBUS, OHIO

Library of Congress Catalog Card Number: 64-17186

First printing .... April 1964

Second printing .... June 1964

Third printing .... March 1965

Fourth printing .... February 1966

Fifth printing .... December 1966

PUBLISHED IN THE UNITED STATES OF AMERICA

TABLE OF CONTENTS

INTRODUCTION

The purpose of this book is to provide both the experienced and the prospective teacher with materials which might lead to a better understanding of:

—the purpose and limitations of phonics instruction as it relates to teaching reading

—concrete practices which may be followed in teaching the various "steps" in phonic analysis

—the rationale which underlies particular instructional practices.

The material in the book reflects several premises:

1. Teaching phonics is an important part of teaching reading.
2. Teachers should be knowledgeable about the purpose of phonic instruction as it relates to reading (*what* to teach) and about the rationale or justification for the practices they follow.
3. There are a number of psychologically sound principles which should be followed in phonics instruction.
4. In recent years, there has been no legitimate basis for a debate on phonetic methods *vs.* sight-word methods, as these terms actually have no identifiable referents.

5. The spurious debate on the above polar positions has tended to obscure real educational issues such as:

a) the proper concentration of analysis that is desirable for the beginning reading period

b) the desirability of teaching rules or generalizations which have very limited applications

c) the logical order in which the "steps" in phonics instruction should be introduced.

As teachers, we need to be well informed about both what to teach and why we teach as we do. Otherwise, methodology may become separated from logical principles of learning. In recent years this has actually happened in much of the discussion of phonics as well as in practices advocated by certain critics of present day reading instruction.

Chapter 1

The Purpose and Limitations of Phonics Instruction

The purpose of phonics instruction, as it relates to reading, is to provide the reader with the ability to pronounce or to approximate the pronunciation of any word he meets in reading, which HE DOES NOT KNOW AS A SIGHT WORD. This is ample reason for teaching phonics, and sufficient justification for teaching it well. The application of phonic analysis in reading situations is simply utilizing one important reading skill. Phonics does not constitute a total method for teaching the complicated process called reading. To keep the teaching of phonics in proper perspective, one must: (1) see phonic analysis as an important reading skill; (2) realize that phonics is only one of a number of ways a child may "solve" words not known as sight words.

In recent years, noticeable confusion has accompanied discussion of reading because the meaning of some of the terms used in that discussion were vague or misleading. Certain critics of reading instruction tried to establish the existence of a dichotomy in which reading instruction was attempted by means of teaching exclusively either "sight words" or phonics. Linguists have rightly pointed out that the terms "phonics" and "phonetics" are often used interchangeably despite the fact that these terms have quite different meanings. In an effort to militate against further confusion, a few brief definitions of basic terms are presented here:

1. *Phonics*—A facet of reading instruction teaching speech sounds of letters and groups of letters in words.

2. *Phonic analysis*—The process of sounding letters or letter combinations to arrive at the pronunciation of words.

3. *Phonetics*—That segment of linguistic science which deals with speech sounds, how these sounds are made vocally, sound changes which develop in languages, and the relation of speech sounds to the total language process. All phonics instruction is derived from phonetics, but phonics (as it relates to reading) utilizes only a relatively small portion of the body of knowledge identified as phonetics.

4. *Word analysis*—An inclusive term which includes all methods of recognizing words which are not known as sight words.

5. *Sight-word method*—The term "sight-word method" is an abstraction which does not adequately describe present-day reading instruction. However, most beginning instruction involves the teaching of a limited number of sight words before phonic analysis is introduced. The term came into common usage because it does describe this first and important step. Gradually, "sight-word method" was used to imply the existence of an instructional approach which proscribed phonics and advocated teaching every new word by sight only.

6. *Phonetic method*—Since there is no exclusive phonic method of teaching reading, this term sometimes functions as either an abstraction or overstatement. For example, if "phonetic method" simply means that phonic analysis is employed, all methods of teaching reading would qualify as phonetic methods. On the other hand, if "phonetic method" implies teaching reading by means of exclusive reliance on phonic analysis, all presently acceptable definitions of "reading" would have to be discarded. "Word analysis" could be substituted for "reading" and children could be punished each time a word was learned as a sight word. Also, English word spellings would have to be completely revised along phonetic principles. This has been suggested in some quarters; but, while this has certain merits, no wholesale revision has as yet been accepted.

7. *Phonetic method* vs. *sight-word method*—These terms are often used to suggest that there presently exist two antithetical approaches to teaching reading. In reality, no such dichotomy exists and teachers of reading should not use these terms in this sense. Nor should critics who use them in this sense go unchallenged.

WORD-ANALYSIS SKILLS

Seeing phonics in proper perspective involves: (1) understanding that phonic analysis is one of several means by which children can "solve" words not known as sight words; (2) noting that phonics relates to, and interacts with, all of the other methods of word analysis such as:

1. *Word form*—In general, all words can be said to be unique in appearance. Yet, in the experience of a primary-level child, the visual forms of words are so much alike that much practice is needed to perceive the minute differences between them. While learning to discriminate word forms, the child might note such limited factors as the length of words, or special features such as *tt*, *ll*, *oo*, or final *y*. Learning to recognize the word *monkey* because it has a tail (y) at the end may serve an immediate and limited purpose; but soon the child will meet *money, merry, funny,* and *penny*. The word *look* may be learned as having two eyes in the middle; but soon the child meets *book, stood, flood*. It is obvious that, as the child expands his reading, these "unique" features become common to a large number of words and it becomes necessary to note every letter detail of words.

2. *Structural analysis*—Here, the child may note structural changes which differentiate between words having common roots. Such changes include:

 a) the addition of inflectional endings (-s, -ed, -ing)
 b) modifications resulting when prefixes or suffixes have been added to known roots (pre-, un-, dis-; -tive, -tion, -ment)
 c) combining two words to form compounds (anyone, someplace, sidewalk).

3. *Context clues*—When a child is reading for meaning, the context in which an unknown word is met is useful in suggesting what the word might be. Usually, only a few words could possibly fill out the meaning. For example:

"The boy threw the ball to his _____."

There are probably not more than a half-dozen words which could be inserted in the blank space (friend, mother, playmate, brother, father, sister). Some possibilities would be less logical than others *depending on what has happened in the story prior to this sentence.*

In addition, it must be kept in mind that the child is not taught to rely exclusively on context. He has been taught to look at the initial letter, the first syllable, (and more if needed) in unknown words. As he solves the initial sound in the word, all or most of the otherwise logical possibilities are eliminated. Returning to our example:

> "The boy threw the ball to his s – – – – –."
> s i s – – –."

A number of devices are utilized by authors to provide context clues which help readers solve new words and difficult concepts. One of these is to incorporate a description-definition in the text.

> "They were now traveling through _____ country. It was very hot, there was sand under foot and the wind blew sand in their eyes. There were no streams—no water whatsoever—and no shade trees. The d_____ extended as far as the eye could see."

Other techniques include comparison or contrast, and the use of synonyms or antonyms.

> "At this point the stream flowed very _____ [rapidly]. The water splashed over the rocks and sent up white spray as it moved *swiftly* through the pass."

Solving the pronunciation of an unknown word is facilitated by:

> *a)* the meaning of the total sentence in which the word occurs
> *b)* what has occurred in previously read sentences and sentences which follow—assuming, of course, that the child is "reading for meaning."

4. *Picture clues*—In beginning reading, pictures provide clues to many unknown words (turkey, father, wagon). Pictures are used both to indicate or represent words and to expand concepts. The fact that some children learn to become too dependent on pictures is not a good argument against the use of pictures. Pictures help focus attention on meaning; they

lead one into a story, and where only a limited number of words are known, pictures supplement.

5. *Phonic analysis*—The English alphabet contains twenty-six letters which represent forty-five speech sounds. The difficulty of learning to read English is compounded by this fact—that many letters and letter combinations represent a number of different sounds. Despite this lack of consistency in written English, a person learning to read must associate printed letter symbols with "characteristic speech sounds." The teaching of letter sounds is referred to as "phonics instruction." The various steps in teaching phonics are listed at the end of this chapter and discussed in detail in later chapters.

SKILLS IN COMBINATION

It should be noted that structural and phonic analysis constantly interact. Such pre-fabricated units as *ex-, pre-, dis-, en-, pro-, -ed, -ing, -tive, -ment, -tion,* and the like, when added to words, do produce structural changes. But each of these, and many more, are also phonic units. The pronunciation of prefixes, suffixes and compound words remains quite consistent.

Structural changes in a word will often camouflage clues which the reader may have used in recognizing the root. When a child does not instantly recognize such a new word, he should resort to sounding. For example, a child may know the word *locate,* but not recognize *dislocated,* or *relocating.* Sounding the "parts" will unlock the pronunciation and, since the meaning of the root word is known, the meaning of the new word is grasped.

The above approaches to word analysis are probably not of equal value in learning to read. Different children may learn to rely on one method more than on others; and some approaches, such as unique word form, have limited utility beyond the early stages of learning to read. Facile reading would not result if one went through a series of trial-and-error responses in which only one of the above approaches to word analysis was used. Efficient readers use various methods of word attack simultaneously.

As an example, assume a child is reading the following sentence in which the blank represents an unknown word:

A. "Look, look," said Jack, "look at the _____."

The content of example *A* alone does not provide enough context clues for the reader to solve the unknown word. In *B*, the sentence is shown in a larger context.

B. "I hear a car," said Jack.
"I do not hear a car," said Suzy. "I hear a funny noise."
"I hear a honk-honk," said Jack, "but I do not see a car."
"That noise is in the sky," said Suzy.
Jack pointed at the sky. "Look, look," said Jack. "Look at the g — — — —."
Suzy said, "They are flying south for the winter."

At this point, the background and previous experience of some readers will suggest the unknown word. The context suggests several classes of subjects, such as birds or airplanes, which would be logical. However, in the child's book, the "unknown" is not a blank space—it is a word composed of letters. The sounds which these letters represent have been studied. Even though the word is not known, the child who has been properly taught will note the initial consonant *g*. He will not say "*b*ird" or "*a*irplane" or any other word which does not begin with the *g* sound. He will "sound" as much as he needs:

"Look at the g — — — —.
gee — —.
geese."

This story, since it is at the primary level, is accompanied by a picture which shows both children looking up — Jack pointing — toward the sky to a *V* formation of geese. Thus, context; previous experience, a picture, sounding the initial consonant, then the double vowel—if needed —all provide clues which will help the reader solve the unknown word without a noticeable hesitation. The less facile reader might require a pause in his reading while he "sounds out" the word. Only a very inefficient reader would depend entirely on "sounding." This would involve wasting all of the other clues—and brings us to our next point.

OVERRELIANCE ON SOUNDING IS NOT EFFICIENT

This discussion of phonics in proper perspective rests on these premises:

1. A reader is handicapped when he has not mastered the sounding techniques he needs to solve words not recognized as sight words.

2. The reader is handicapped if he relies *too heavily* on phonic analysis WHEN OTHER MODES OF ATTACK WOULD BE MORE ECONOMICAL. If a child CAN sound every word in a story and DOES sound every word, he is, in all probability, an inefficient reader. Each interruption of the reading process by *phonic analysis of a word* detracts from smooth, fluent reading.

3. Early reading instruction can be structured so as to inculcate any one of a number of "sets." A child may overlearn the habit of sounding. He may still be analyzing words long after he should have mastered them as sight words. That is, he may be sounding words the tenth, twentieth or fiftieth time he meets them. Since the objective of reading instruction is not to produce this kind of reader, every effort should be made to see that the child does not generalize that "sounding out words is reading."

4. Efficient reading involves developing the ability to analyze or sound unknown words, but at the same time holding reliance on such analysis to an absolute minimum.

VARIABILITY OF LETTER SOUNDS IN ENGLISH

One factor which limits the efficacy of phonic analysis in learning to read English is the fact that the pronunciation of English words does not follow any consistent patterns. Although English is an alphabetic language in its written form, it is also one of the least phonetically lawful. That is, there is nothing like a one-to-one relationship between letter spellings and letter sounds in English. Some of the reasons which account in part for this fact are:

1. Many words have come into English from other languages—such as Latin, Greek, French and German (*waive, alias, corps, debris, alien, buoy, feint, bouquet,* etc.).

2. A given letter, or letters, may have many different sounds in different words (*cow* [ow]; *low* [ō]; *can* [ă]; *cane* [ā]; *cap* [k]; *city* [s]; *bus* [s]; *his* [z]; *measure* [zh]).

3. In thousands of English words, a letter or letters may have no sound (knbw, kick, listen, light, plumb, wring).

The following examples illustrate some of the variability found in English words. Some words are:

> pronounced the same,
> spelled differently,
> and each is phonetically "lawful."

sail—sale; meat—meet; heal—heel; maid—made

In these examples, the generalization which applies to both spellings is:

When there are two vowels in a word, usually the first is long and the second is silent.

In the following, one word in each pair is governed by the phonic generalization listed above—the *other* is not.

ate	rain	peace	wait
eight	reign	piece	weight

A word may have one or more *silent letters* which differentiates it from another word which is pronounced exactly the same:

rap	our	no	night	plum
wrap	hour	know	knight	plumb

Some words are spelled exactly the same but have different origins, meanings, and pronunciations.

"Your mother will *object* if you keep this *object* in your room."
"The author was *content* with the *content* of his story."

The long sound of vowels may be "made" by any of these and other combinations in words:

$\bar{a} =$	day *ay*	they *ey*	fate *a* (e)	sail *ai*	reign *ei*	great *ea*	
$\bar{e} =$	feet *ee*	meat *ea*	deceive *ei*	brief *ie*	ski *i*	key *ey*	
$\bar{\imath} =$	my *y*	kite *i* (e)	pie *ie*	height *ei*	buy *uy*	guide *ui*	
$\bar{o} =$	show *ow*	hold *o* (+ld)	boat *oa*	note *o* (e)	go *o*	door *oo*	four *ou*
$\bar{u} =$	flew *ew*	view *iew*	tube *u*	due *ue*	suit *ui*	you *"*	

It should be evident from the above that it would not be easy to write a series of rules to cover the sounds that letters make in the English language. In fact, there *is no phonic rule* which will apply to all words which meet the criteria the rule sets forth. Therefore, any phonic rule may have to be "amended" many times to cover the situations the original rule was designed to cover. As an example, let us look at the most widely applicable rule relating to vowel sounds:

A single vowel in medial position, in a word or syllable, usually has its short sound.

This generalization is quite useful to children learning to read. Studies of the frequency with which it applies to words met in primary reading support the view that it should be taught.[1] However, it should also be pointed out that there are a great number of instances in which the generalization does not hold. The following are examples of exceptions followed by generalizations which have emerged to cover these situations.

Exception A:	hold, cold, bold, gold, bolt, colt.
New rule:	The single vowel *o*, followed by *ld* or *lt*, has its long sound.
Exception B:	*car, fir, fur, her, for, part, bird, hurt, perch, corn,* etc.
New rule:	A vowel followed by *r* has neither its long nor short sound—the vowel sound is modified by the *r*.
Exception C:	*wild, mild, child; find, kind, mind, blind,* etc.
New rule:	The vowel *i* before *ld* or *nd* is usually long.
Exception D:	*fall, call, ball,* etc.; *salt, malt, halt.*
New rule:	The vowel *a* followed by *ll* or *lt*, has a pronunciation like *aw* (ball = bawl).
Exception E:	*high, sigh; light, night, bright, flight,* etc.
New rule:	The vowel *i* in *igh* or *ight* words is usually long.
Other exceptions:	sign = (i); was = (uz); both = (ō); front = (u).

---

[1] Ruth E. Oakes, "A Study of the Vowel Situations in a Primary Vocabulary," *Education*, LXXII (May, 1952), 604-17; and Theodore Clymer, "The Utility of Phonic Generalizations in the Primary Grades," *The Reading Teacher*, XVI (January, 1963), 252-58.

These illustrations have dealt only with monosyllabic words containing a single vowel in medial position. The "exceptions" to the basic rule are only the major ones which might logically be dealt with in teaching reading, and the words listed represent only a small fraction of those that could be cited.

The point of this discussion is not to attempt to refute the premise stated earlier that "there is ample reason for teaching phonics—and teaching it well," but rather to suggest that phonics has its limitations when applied to learning to read English. In a number of different sources, one might read that 85 per cent of English words are phonetic. It is not clear what this statement means; but it probably was meant to imply the possibility of formulating enough phonic rules to cover approximately this percentage of English words. As rules become more involved and cover fewer and fewer actual words, one may question the relationship between learning these rules and learning the process called "reading."

The discussion of the purpose and limitations of phonics in reading instruction is summarized with a restatement of premises:

1. Phonic analysis is taught in order that children may pronounce words they do not recognize as sight words.

2. This skill is needed if children are to become independent readers —thus, teaching phonics is an important facet of teaching reading.

3. Phonics is only one method of *word analysis*. Facile readers use many methods, often in combination.

4. Despite the values in teaching and learning phonic analysis, too much reliance on phonic analysis inhibits facile reading.

5. The nature of the English language imposes limitations on the degree to which formal instruction in phonic analysis can aid the beginning reader.

EDUCATIONAL ISSUES IN TEACHING PHONICS

Most of the individuals engaged in the on-going debate on teaching reading would probably not take exception to the points listed above; however, one corps of critics of present reading instruction has been able to focus the attention of the public on a spurious issue—*phonetic method* vs. *sight-word method*. The idea has been planted that the term "sight-word method" actually describes present methodology; that in this method, all words introduced at various instructional levels are taught as sight words; and that phonics is neither advocated nor used in reading instruction. None of this fits the facts. However, if one starts from the premise that this idea is factual, the real methodological issues related to phonics instruction are neatly covered up. A few of the educational issues which merit the attention of teachers are:

1. Should beginning reading instruction start with teaching *whole words* as *units*—or with teaching the sounds letters make in words?

2. How much phonics should be included in beginning reading; i.e., in grade one?

3. In what sequence or order should the steps in phonics be taught?

THE RATIONALE FOR TEACHING WHOLE WORDS FIRST

A child entering school has had much experience in *hearing* and in *speaking* or using language. He has learned oral language in units of words—he has associated meaning with whole words and with words used in combination. Some linguists stress that language IS oral and that the language usage of the preschool child implies the ability to discriminate the letter sounds heard in words. This is much too facile a generalization to apply to a five- or six-year-old's meaningful use of oral language. The child has not mastered the sophisticated knowledge of speech sounds that the linguist's statement implies. To the child, the spoken equivalent of *cat* is a unitary or global sound which he can differentiate globally from all other language units called words.

Beginning reading involves associating unknown printed word symbols with the known oral language or speech equivalents of *words*. There is a one-to-one relationship between the pronunciation of words and the printed word symbol. The oral statement, "The eight knights knew night would come," is depicted in printed symbols:

"The eight knights knew night would come."

Phonetically this would be written:

"The āt nītz nū nīt wúd kŭm."

In augmented Roman, it would appear:

ʄhe æt nietz nue niet wwd cum

The following points are those frequently cited as justification for teaching whole words as units prior to teaching phonic analysis of letter sounds:

1. The child's knowledge of, and use of, oral language involves the meaningful use of words and of words in combination. We wish the learner to move one short step from what is known—to what is to be learned. Learning printed whole words is a logical *first step* in the reading process.

2. Spoken language and printed word symbols maintain a one-to-one relationship, *regardless of the gross spelling irregularities found in English*. However, the sounds contributed by individual letters in printed words vary tremendously.

3. Reading is a more meaningful process when the child deals with whole words as units, rather than with letter sounds. Meaning resides in the total word and in the special ways words are used together—not in the sound of the individual letter-parts of words.

4. If a child knows a number of words as sight words, he can more easily be taught to *see* and *hear* similarities between the known words and new words he meets.

5. As the first step in beginning reading, it is easier to learn a number of sight words than to learn a set of complicated rules for sounding out letters in words.

6. Many words met in beginning reading do not lend themselves to phonic analysis. These should be learned as sight words.

7. The objective of reading instruction is not to have the child analyze each word. However, if in beginning instruction he is taught to analyze each word, this habit will be acquired.

8. Learning whole words teaches children to look at the whole word from left to right, as opposed to some phonic systems which advocate teaching vowel sounds first. In a vast majority of words, this mode of attack will start the analysis in the middle of words, rather than at the beginning of the word.

AMOUNT OF PHONICS TAUGHT IN BEGINNING READING INSTRUCTION

This is one of the most important issues related to phonics instruction. All methods and materials used in present-day reading instruction advocate teaching much the same program of phonics during the primary years. However, there are important differences as to how this phonics instruction is spaced throughout this period. One approach, which might be labeled "early emphasis on phonic instruction," advocates using the first eight weeks of formal reading instruction for teaching letter sounds, both vowels and consonants. Furthermore, the grade-one program is highly saturated with analysis—at least 80 per cent of the entire phonics program being introduced in grade one.

A quite different point of view holds that the child's first experiences with reading should be meaningful and deal with words rather than letter sounds. The grade-one program of phonic analysis teaches all consonant sounds, consonant blends, some inflectional endings, and some compounds. The major differences in philosophy and practice in these two instructional approaches are outlined below:

Early emphasis on phonic analysis	*Early emphasis on reading for meaning*
A. Teach sound of letters before child learns words.	A. Teach some words as sight words — then analyze speech sounds heard in these known words.
B. Teach phonic analysis from beginning of reading instruction; considerable emphasis in early stages of instruction.	B. Learn words as wholes. Read words in sentences and stories; no emphasis on "analysis" in early stages of instruction.
C. Introduce most (70-85 per cent) of phonic rules on principles in grade one.	C. Teach much smaller per cent of rules or principles in grade one.
D. Introduction of total phonics program is completed in grade two. Reviewed throughout grades two and three.	D. Total phonics program taught over time period of grades one, two, and three.

(See Figure 1)

FIGURE 1

Area under curves represents number of phonic principles or rules introduced at various grade levels. (Does not refer to amount of classroom time devoted to instruction.)

Early emphasis on phonics: Early emphasis on whole-words and meaning:

dotted line . . . .   solid line_____.

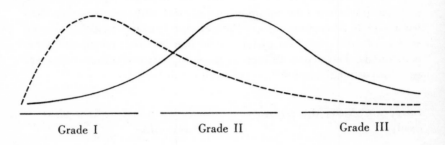

| Grade I | Grade II | Grade III |

THE ORDER IN WHICH PHONIC SKILLS ARE TAUGHT

The third issue is the sequence in which the various steps in the phonics program should be introduced and taught. This is not an important problem in certain contexts, such as: In what order should consonant sounds be taught; which vowel sound should be taught first; should all long vowel sounds be taught before short vowel sounds (or vice versa) ; which consonant blends should be taught first?

However, the question of whether to introduce the teaching of phonics by teaching consonant sounds first or vowel sounds first is worthy of some discussion. There is little question that children can learn these skills in either order. The questions which teachers should answer are:

1. What are the data related to this issue of the proper sequence for teaching the various steps in phonics?

2. Are the procedures which I follow supported by sound learning theory?

The following discussion examines a number of the justifications commonly advanced by proponents of teaching consonant sounds first and by those who support teaching vowel sounds first.

Rationale for Teaching Consonant Sounds First

1. The majority of words children meet in beginning reading are words which begin with consonants. For instance, 175 (or approximately 80 per cent) of the 220 words on the Dolch Basic Sight Word Test[2] begin with consonants. The Dale List of 769 Easy Words[3] contains even a higher proportion (87 per cent) of words beginning with consonants.

2. It is good learning theory to have the child start phonic analysis with the beginning of words, working his way through the words from left to right. This reinforces the practice of reading from left to right and focuses the child's attention on the first part of the word. This is essential for facile reading, and an absolute prerequisite if he is to *solve* the word by "sounding."

3. Consonants tend to be much more consistent than vowels in sound representation. For instance, eleven consonants (j, k, l, m, n, p, b, h, r, v, w) have only one sound each. Certain other consonants which have two sounds present no problem in BEGINNING reading instruction because one of the two basic sounds can be left until the child has had some considerable practice in reading. Examples:

> *c* = *k* in *cat, cake, color, cup, cap, cut, could, can, cold, cry, call, clean, cage*

> *c* = *s* when *c* is followed by *e, i,* or *y* (cent, century, ceiling, cypress, celebrate, citizen, cycle, cease)

> *d* has *d* sound in *did, doll, don't, day, do, dog, dish*

> *d* has *j* sound in *individual, graduate, cordial*

Rationale for Teaching Vowel Sounds First

1. Beginning readers can learn vowel sounds. The more quickly they learn them, the more quickly they will become independent readers. (It

---

[2] Obtainable from The Garrard Press, Champaign, Illinois.

[3] Edgar Dale, "A Comparison of Two Word Lists," *Educational Research Bulletin,* (December 9, 1931), 484–89.

will be noted that this statement is equally valid when applied to consonants.)

2. Beginning phonic analysis with vowel sounds, it is stated, is justifiable because vowels carry more of a clue to the word's pronunciation than do consonants. This theory is often questioned on the basis that it is simply not supported by the evidence.[4] Assume the following blank space represents a missing vowel: l–ck. There are only four possibilities —lack, lick, lock, luck. Insert each of these vowels, but leave the initial consonant blank and a much larger number of possibilities results:

–ack	–ick	–ock	–uck
*b*ack	*D*ick	*c*ock	*b*uck
*h*ack	*k*ick	*d*ock	*d*uck
*J*ack	*h*ick	*l*ock	*h*uck
*l*ack	*l*ick	*m*ock	*l*uck
*M*ack	*p*ick	*r*ock	*m*uck
*p*ack	*s*ick	*s*ock	*p*uck
*r*ack	*t*ick		*s*uck
*s*ack	*w*ick		*t*uck

The same holds for double vowels:

–eed can be *s*eed *w*eed *n*eed *r*eed *d*eed *f*eed *h*eed
–eat can be *m*eat *h*eat *n*eat *p*eat *s*eat *f*eat *b*eat
–ail can be *t*ail *m*ail *b*ail *f*ail *p*ail *r*ail *n*ail

3. Vowels should be taught first because all words (and syllables) contain vowels. If the words *a, I,* and *eye* are eliminated, one may demonstrate that all words also contain consonants. How the fact that all words contain vowels is a justification for teaching vowel sounds first has not been explained in any material which has come to the writer's attention.

In conclusion, it would appear that certain facts—(1) consonants are consistent in their sound; (2) the vast majority of words begin with consonants; (3) children should learn to read English from left to right

---

[4] William S. Gray, *On Their Own in Reading* (Chicago: Scott, Foresman & Company, 1960), pp. 35–36.

and analyze words left to right—offer a substantial basis for teaching consonants first.

PRINCIPLES TO APPLY IN TEACHING PHONICS

The systematic study of any teaching-learning situation may be expected to yield a set of psychologically sound principles which relate to and govern teaching procedures. In teaching, one would follow sound principles in order to enhance learning. Principles do not spell out precise practices to be followed, but rather provide a set of guidelines by which to measure classroom instructional practices. The following principles for teaching *phonic analysis* are advanced for teachers' consideration. If these principles are found to be educationally sound, they merit application in the classroom.

1. *For any child to profit from systematic instruction in phonics, he must have the ability to discriminate between similar speech sounds.* To attempt to teach numerous phonic generalizations in the absence of auditory discrimination equal to the learning task is not only inadvisable from the standpoint of learning, but is often detrimental to the learner.

2. *Auditory and visual training should be blended and taught simultaneously.* Phonics (as it relates to reading) is teaching speech-sound equivalents for printed letters and letter combinations. Thus, a child must be able to recognize instantly and discriminate visually between printed letter symbols before instruction in phonics can have any relation to reading printed symbols. For example, a child who can differentiate between the sounds of *bee* and *dee,* but cannot visually discriminate between the printed symbols *b* and *d* cannot apply phonics in a reading situation which involves words containing these symbols.

3. *Any instructional practice which produces a learning set, which in itself inhibits the development of reading for meaning, merits reappraisal.* If reading is "getting meaning," children should not be conditioned in beginning reading instruction to equate reading with "sounding" or "word analysis." Practices followed in beginning reading instruction DO inculcate a "set" in the learner. In the golden age of phonics, many children DID develop the set that pronouncing words was reading. Sounding out words is a needed skill, but the facile reader will apply it only when nec-

essary; and the less analysis that is needed in a given reading situation, the more efficient and meaningful will be the reading. A third-grade child who CAN sound every word on a page and DOES sound every word on the page is an impaired reader. Since we do not wish to produce this type of reader, we should assiduously avoid practices which lead to this type of development.

4. *All phonic facts and generalizations necessary for a child to become an independent reader should be taught.*

5. *For a child to learn to read, it is not necessary for him to learn phonic generalizations which have extremely limited application.* A teacher accepting this principle would still have to arrive at a conclusion as to what rules actually fit under this classification. Individual teachers may resolve this problem by answering questions such as the following in regard to each phonic generalization they propose to teach:

a) What contribution will this generalization make in the "learning-to-read process?"

b) Does this generalization apply to enough words which the child will meet in his current reading program to justify my teaching it NOW?

6. *Instructional practice which leads to overreliance on one method of word attack is indefensible.* In any reading situation, words appear in context; many words have prefabricated sound-sight units such as prefixes, suffixes, inflectional endings, and roots combined in compounds. To teach reliance on context clues alone would be inadequate, and to rely on "sounding" while ignoring all other clues would be equally indefensible. It is wasteful not to attack an unknown word simultaneously on every possible front.

7. *All elementary teachers should be familiar with the entire phonics program.* All teachers of reading, regardless of grade level, will probably find it necessary to teach, review, or reteach certain phonic skills to some children in their classrooms. Thus, familiarity with all steps in phonics instruction is essential.

8. *A thorough and on-going diagnosis of each child's needs and present knowledge is a prerequisite for following sound principles of teaching phonic skills.* It is not desirable to teach more phonics than a given child needs, or to omit teaching needed skills not yet mastered. *Diagnosis is the key to achieving this proper balance.*

9. *Knowledge of phonic generalizations (rules) does not assure ability to apply these generalizations in reading situations.* Both in teaching and learning, the process of "sounding out words" must be differentiated from learning rules. Some children can recite a given rule and yet have no ability to apply or practice what it tells them to do. On the other hand, knowledge of phonic generalizations *is* useful to children. In general, material should be presented in such a way that the application of a given generalization evolves out of actual word study. At best, phonic generalizations are a crutch which may have utility at certain points on the learning continuum. A reader who is continually groping for a rule to apply when he meets a word not known as a sight word is not a facile reader.

STEPS IN TEACHING PHONICS

The outline below lists the steps in the order in which they are discussed in the following chapters.

1. Auditory-visual discrimination

2. Teaching consonant sounds
   a) Initial consonants
   b) Consonant digraphs (sh, wh, th, ch)
   c) Consonant blends (br, cl, str, etc.)
   d) Substituting initial consonant sounds
   e) Sounding consonants at end of words
   f) Consonant digraphs (nk, ng, ck, qu)
   g) Consonant irregularities
   h) Silent consonants
   i) Sight-word list—non-phonetic spellings
   j) Contractions

3. Teaching vowel sounds
   a) Short vowel sounds
   b) Long vowel sounds
   c) Teaching long and short sounds together
   d) Exceptions to vowel rules taught
   e) Diphthongs
   f) Sounds of $\bar{oo}$ and $\breve{oo}$

4. Syllabication
   a) Rules
   b) Prefixes and suffixes
   c) Compound words
   d) Doubling final consonants
   e) Accent

These steps in phonic analysis represent a series of instructional tasks which merit inclusion in reading instruction. It is suggested that these steps be taught in the order in which they are presented. This is believed to be a logical sequence, but it is not implied that this is the only defensible sequence.

It will be noted that the steps listed are only a bare outline of major facets of instruction. For instance, teaching consonant sounds is one step, but it involves at least two-dozen separate teachings (since some consonants have more than one sound). Teaching consonant digraphs and blends would include another thirty separate tasks. All steps must be reviewed and retaught as needed. Diagnosis of individual pupils' progress will determine when, and how much, review is necessary.

Chapter 2

Teaching Auditory-Visual Discrimination and Consonant Sounds

PHONICS INSTRUCTION RELATED TO PREVIOUS LEARNINGS

Learning to read involves the ability to make finer and finer discriminations between word symbols which are very much alike, as well as the association of oral speech sounds with printed letters and letter combinations. These are often referred to as "mechanical" skills in the reading process and are sometimes contrasted with "comprehension" skills. To establish such a dichotomy may be convenient in a discussion of reading, but it should not be forgotten that no reading can take place in the absence of the discrimination skills just mentioned. Fortunately, the child, before beginning to read, has had many experiences which bear directly on this important learning task.

The most important of these previous experiences deals with language usage. The child upon entering school:

1. can differentiate between thousands of words when he hears them spoken by other individuals
2. can use thousands of words himself (speak)
3. has "concepts" for thousands of words.

These are the language skills which are related to learning to read. Two new skills must be developed—visual recognition of printed words, and association of known speech sounds with printed letters and letter combinations. The following material illustrates a number of approaches for teaching or developing auditory and visual discrimination.

TEACHING AUDITORY DISCRIMINATION

Premise: The successful teaching of all subsequent steps in phonic analysis is based on the child's ability to discriminate between speech sounds *in words*. The ability to make or use all of the sounds found in English does not assure that an individual can actually discriminate between certain sets of very similar sounds. Phonics instruction aims at instant association of a particular sound with a given letter or letters. Thus, if a child cannot distinguish the minute auditory differences being taught in a particular phonics lesson, he cannot profit from that instruction.

Occasionally, children are fairly successful in learning consonant sounds but have trouble in mastering certain vowel sounds. An example of such a case is a high-school student who could not differentiate between spoken words containing the short sound of *e* or *i*. Pairs of words, which differed only as to the vowel in medial position, were numbered for identification purposes. The tutor would say one of the words and ask the boy to give the number of the word pronounced. His responses demonstrated conclusively that he could not aurally distinguish between words such as the following:

A.	(1) bet	(2) bit		D.	(1) pen	(2) pin
B.	(1) Ben	(2) bin		E.	(1) bed	(2) bid
C.	(1) mitt	(2) met		F.	(1) then	(2) thin

Many hours of practice were required for this boy to overcome this deficiency. A tape recorder was used as the tutor and boy read words from identical lists. The tutor would pronounce a word, then the boy would say the same word using the tutor's pronunciation as a model. The student listened to these recordings many times before he was able to differentiate between the vowel sounds.

The procedures which a teacher might use in helping children develop skill in auditory discrimination are practically unlimited. The following are illustrative:

1. Children listen while the teacher pronounces a series of words, all of which begin with the same consonant sound: *b*elt, *b*all, *b*ird, *b*e, *b*one. Children then volunteer other words which begin with the same sound: *b*aby, *b*ug, *b*at, *b*oom, *b*ang.

2. A number of pictures are collected from workbooks, catalogues, or magazines. Paste each picture on a separate piece of cardboard to make handling easier. The child is to arrange these into groups on the basis of the initial sound of the NAME of the objects pictured. That is, pictures of *baby, ball, boat,* are put in one group; pictures of *house, hand, horse,* in another.

3. "What sound do we hear?"

   a) Secure a number of pictures of objects with which children characteristically associate particular sounds.

   b) Paste each picture on a separate piece of cardboard.

   c) As each picture is shown, ask a selected child, or the group, "to make the sound that this object makes."

FIGURE 2

clock	lamb	bass drum	bee	duck	telephone
tick-tock	baa-baa	boom-boom	buzz-buzz	quack-quack	ting-a-ling

4. Practice in hearing like sounds which conclude words (rhymes).

   a) Teacher pronounces two words.

   b) If the words rhyme, (mill—hill) the children clap their hands once. If the words do not rhyme, (make—milk) children say "no."

   drum—hum; boom—bang; cap—mad; bake—cake; small—tall; fan—man; sit—hit; cold—gold

5. Secure pictures which contain many objects (advertisements, etc.).

TEACHER: "Do you see an object which begins with the sound we hear at the beginning of the names *B*illy and *B*etty?"
(*b*all—*b*asket)

"Do you see a picture of something which begins with the sound we hear at the beginning of the words *h*and and *h*elp?"

(*h*at—*h*orse)—Continue to use sounds illustrated in picture.

TEACHING VISUAL DISCRIMINATION

Teaching the association of the sound of letters and combination of letters with the printed symbol equivalents is dependent on the child's ability to recognize and discriminate visually between printed letters: "*b*ad"—"*d*ad"; "*m*oon"—"*n*oon"; "b*a*t"—"b*i*t"—"b*u*t"—"b*e*t," and the like. Illustrative examples of teaching visual discrimination in reading situations follow:

1. Provide the child with practice in *seeing* identical letter patterns in different words.

> *a*) *b*all, *b*aby, *b*ird, *b*elt
> "What do you see at the beginning of each of these words?"
> "Yes, they all begin the same—with the letter *b*. Look at the word closely and LISTEN to the sound of *b* at the beginning of each word." (Pronounce words slowly—moving from left to right.)
>
> *b*) *h*all, *c*all, *f*all, *t*all
> (Call attention to visual pattern at the end of each word—pronounce and listen to the sound.)
>
> *c*) *bl*ack, *bl*ock, *bl*ue, *bl*ow

2. Mark each word that begins with the same italicized letter(s) as those in the first word.

*m*ake:	move	after	must	lake
*t*all:	make	take	best	took
*bl*ock:	laugh	blow	farm	blue
*ch*ange:	child	came	chair	could
*sh*ow:	stage	shine	short	year

(Do not work with blends or digraphs until single initial consonant sounds have been taught.)

3. In the following exercise, the teacher reads the sentences. The child should know the letter-name and sound of the stimulus letters *b* and *m*. Children provide the missing words from context plus the initial-letter clue.

> "Children read b_____."
> "Boys play   b_____."
> "Cats like   m_____."
> "Milk costs   m_____."

4. Match words with beginning sound of pictured items: "Underline the words which begin with the same sound as the picture object."

FIGURE 3

lake
boat
box
rose
bench

cat
fall
car
called
seen

The preceding discussion points up the fact that auditory discrimination can be taught before children attempt to read. However, auditory discrimination in a reading situation is inevitably tied to visual recognition of letter symbols. Therefore, auditory-visual skills should be practiced simultaneously.

TEACHING CONSONANT SOUNDS

The following points briefly restate the rationale for teaching consonant sounds before vowel sounds.

1. The majority of words children meet in beginning reading start with consonants.

2. It is desirable that children learning to read look at the beginning of a word first; and, if phonic analysis is necessary, it should begin with the first part of the word.

3. The consonant sounds are much more constant than vowel sounds. When children learn the sound of a given consonant, this sound will "hold" in most words the child meets.

Assuming the child has learned a few sight words, he will *know* some printed word symbols which begin with any given consonant. The first consonant sounds taught might be those which have only one sound; such as *b, m, r, p, l, h, k, v, j, n,* and *f*. One could also teach the most common sounds of consonants *t* and *c*, ignoring for the moment, endings *-tion* and *-tive*. While the order in which consonant sounds are taught is not of crucial importance, logic might suggest that *z, x, q (qu), g* with sound of *j*, etc., might be the last sounds taught.

CONSONANTS IN INITIAL POSITION

For the purposes of illustration, the steps in teaching the sound of the consonant *b* (Approach 1) are given in detail. All other consonant sounds may be taught in the same manner. Approach 2 illustrates the use of pictured objects to teach the sound of *f, b,* and hard sound of *c*.

a) Print the letter *b* (upper and lower case) on the chalkboard. Indicate that for the next few minutes the group will study the sound of

APPROACH 1

B	b
	baby
	ball
	be
	boy
	Betty
	Billy

the letter *b*, as heard in words. Write a column of previously studied words, all of which begin with the letter *b*, on the board.

b) Any words the children have met as sight words in experience charts or other materials may be used—words such as *baby, ball, be, boy*—also, familiar names of children in the class—*Betty, Billy*, etc.—which call for capital letters.

c) Ask the children to look at the words carefully and name the letter that begins each word. Indicate that a big *B* or capital letter is used in names.

d) As the teacher pronounces the words, the children are asked to *listen* to the sound heard at the beginning of each word. The initial sound is emphasized but not distorted.

e) The children are then invited to read the words in unison, listening carefully to the sound of *b* as they say the words.

f) Ask children to supply other words which begin with the sound of *b* as heard in "*baby*," "*ball*," etc. (Accept any words which begin with *b*—even words with the initial blend sounds as in blue, blow, brown, etc. You may not wish to add the blend words to the list on the board, but you may add others such as book, box, both, buy, but, bat, basket.)

g) Children have not been asked to ISOLATE and sound the letter *b* as *buh*. They hear the sound of *b* as it occurs in words. The word *bat* is not sounded out *buh-ah-tuh* = *bat*. The word *bat* is a one-syllable, not a three-syllable, word. Emphasis is justifiable—distortion is not.

APPROACH 2

Drill on discrimination may be accomplished through the use of pictures. Assume preliminary board work (as illustrated above) has introduced the sounds of *b*, hard *c*, and *f*. A number of pictures may be secured from magazines, catalogues, and workbooks. Each picture may be pasted on cardboard or oak tag for easier handling. One stimulus picture for each of the initial sounds of *b*, *c*, *f* is selected (book, cat, fish). Children place all of the pictures which begin with a given sound into piles, boxes, or envelopes. (See Figure 4.)

It will be noted in Approach 2 that the child does not have visual clues provided by the initial letter of printed words (bell, boat, bear, bed, ball). He must *pronounce* the name of the pictured object and *hear* the initial sound. Many exercises which purport to exercise or test auditory discrimination can be worked successfully by relying entirely on visual cues.

FIGURE 4

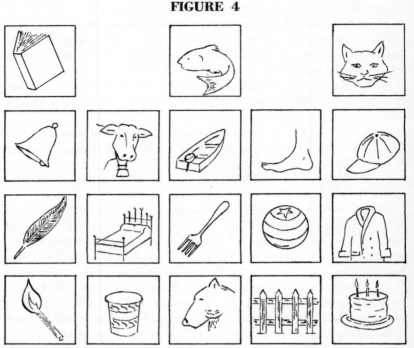

Figure 5 is such an exercise. A picture of a familiar object is shown along with the name of the object (bird).

The child is to underline all of the words which begin with the same *sound* as the stimulus word and pictured object. This exercise is useful only if the child actually "sounds out" and listens carefully to the initial sound heard in each instance. If he simply recognizes *visually* that *baby* starts with the same letter as *bird,* he may do the exercise correctly, yet receive no practice in auditory discrimination.

To avoid undesirable repetition, the step-by-step teaching of other initial consonants will not be presented. A list of easier words which might be used in board work for teaching each of the other consonant sounds is presented in Table 5 at the end of this chapter. As long as the initial sound is constant the words used for illustrative purposes do not need to be phonetic throughout—many are sight words.

FIGURE 5

TEACHING CONSONANT DIGRAPHS (SH, WH, TH, CH)

Digraphs are combinations of two letters which result in one speech sound. The sound heard is not a blend of the two letters involved, but is a completely new sound. A given digraph may have more than one pronunciation but the letter combination results in a single sound in each case (*ch* = *k* in"*ch*orus"; *sh* in "*ch*ef"; *ch* in "*ch*urch"). Digraphs may be taught in a manner similar to that used for teaching consonant sounds.

SHALL

SHE

SHIP

SHOW

STEPS IN BRIEF:

1. Place several stimulus words on the chalkboard.

2. Ask the children to look at the words carefully and note how they are alike. Draw out observation that all words begin with *sh*. (Underline the digraph being taught; i.e., *sh*, *ch*, *th*, *wh*.)

3. Ask the children to listen to the sound of *sh* as they say the words together.

4. Invite children to supply other words which begin with the same sound as "*sh*all," "*sh*e," "*sh*ip," "*sh*ow."

NOTE: The digraph *sh* usually has the sound heard in these stimulus words. Other common *sh* words:

shut, shop, shot, sheep, shape, shade, short, sheet, shoot, shoe, shell, shirt, shovel, shake, sharp, shine

Words ending with *sh* sounds: push, dish, wish, wash.

The digraph *wh* is usually pronounced as if spelled *hw*:
when = hwen; white = hwite. The *wh* sound may be taught as is *sh* above. Other common *wh* words: why, where, wheel, wheat, whisper, whether, whale, whiskers.

WHEN
WHITE
WHAT
WHICH

Exceptions: When *o* follows *wh*, the *w* is silent: who = hōō;   whole = hōl;   whom = hōōm;   whose = hōōz.

The digraph *th* has two common sounds. (The concepts of *voiced* and *unvoiced* need not be taught.)

Voiced th sound as in:				*Unvoiced th sound as in:*			
this	their	they	though	thing	their	thimble	thank
that	then	there	than	them	think	thick	third	thumb

While the consonant digraph *ch* has three different sounds, the most common and the one met almost exclusively in beginning reading is that of *ch* heard in *chair* or *much*:

(Common words for use in teaching exercises)

chair	chin	chose	charm	chalk	ea*ch*	rea*ch*
child	check	chop	chance	cheer	su*ch*	*ch*ur*ch*
chicken	cheek	change	chimney	chief	wat*ch*	much

Much later, children will meet the other sounds of *ch* = *k*, *ch* = *sh*. These need not be taught in beginning reading.

chorus	(ko rus)	chef	(shef)
character	(kar ak ter)	chassis	(shas ĭ)
chemist	(kem ist)	chauffeur	(sho fur)
choir	(kwir)	chic	(shek)
chord	(kord)	chiffon	(shif on)
chrome	(krom)	chamois	(sham ĭ)

TEACHING CONSONANT BLENDS

Consonant blends consist of two or more letters which are blended into a single speech sound. If a child attempts to sound separately each of the consonants in a blend, distortion and confusion will result. Pronouncing the *bl* combination in the word *blue,* does not result in the separate sounds of *b* heard in *but,* or *l* heard in *love.* These letters must be blended to arrive at the correct sound. The child *knows these speech sounds*—he must learn to recognize their printed equivalents. For example, the pupil knows the sound of *s,* as heard in *see, sit, some, say;* and the sound of *t,* as heard in *tell, to talk, top.* The next short step, from the known to the unknown, would be teaching the blend sound *st,* as heard in *stop, still, stand,* and the like.

Two- and three-letter consonant blends may be divided into three major groups on the basis of a common letter:

1. Those in which *r* is the concluding letter (see Column *A*).
2. Those in which *l* is the concluding letter (see Column *B*).
3. Those which begin with the letter *s* (see Column *C*).

Column A		Column B		Column C	
br	scr	bl	spl	sc	str
cr	spr	cl		sk	
dr	str	fl		sm	
fr	thr	gl		sn	
gr		pl		sp	
pr		sl		st	
tr				sw	

The above are arranged in alphabetical order, but may be taught in any order desired. The two-letter blends are easier to learn and occur more frequently in words met in beginning reading than do the three-letter blends. Therefore, the former are taught first.

There are a number of ways to teach children how to master these blend sounds. Regardless of the approach used, the objectives in teaching blends are to have the child:

1. *see* the letter combination involved
2. realize that in every case the letters combine into a blend sound
3. discriminate between the blend sound and the sound of individual letters, i.e., "*pay*," "*lay*," "*play*."

Procedures used in teaching initial blends closely parallel those used in teaching initial consonant sounds. For illustrative purposes the steps in teaching the sound *st* are given in detail (see Procedure 1 below). All other consonant blends may be taught in the same manner. Exercises which provide drill on auditory-visual recognition of blends are illustrated in Procedure 2.

PROCEDURE 1

STOP
STILL
STAR
STAND
STICK

a) Place a few *st* words on the board.

b) Children are asked to look at each word, and attention is directed to the *st* beginning.

c) As the teacher pronounces each word, the pupils are asked to listen to the sound the *st* makes in each word. The words should be pronounced clearly with emphasis on the initial blend sound.

d) The manner in which the *s* and *t* are blended into one sound is emphasized. The sound is the one heard at the beginning of the words *stop, still, star.*

e) Children may be asked to give other words which begin with this sound. (See Table 6). Accept all words given which have the *st* combination. Write any or all suggested words beneath the stimulus words already on the board.

f) Various pupils may go to the board and underline the two letters (st) as they pronounce the words *stop, still,* etc.

Providing Drill on Visual-auditory Recognition of Blends

PROCEDURE 2

After teaching several consonant blends, provide further practice through board work or teacher-made seat-work exercises. (Examples of such exercises are shown below.)

a) Prepare a series of three stimulus words. The teacher pronounces one of the words in each series. Children listen and underline the word the teacher pronounces.

1. blue	2. front	3. *drum*	4. *second*	5. friend
blow	friend	dear	small	family
brake	*farm*	drink	smart	*fright*

6. plant	7. smile	8. black	9. plain	10. dress
plank	smell	*plank*	*plant*	dive
paint	*sailed*	blank	party	*drive*

b) Spell a word correctly by filling in the missing spaces with the blends: fl, st, fr, tr:

– – ain	– – eet	– – esh	– – our	– – oor
– – ake	– – ill	– – are	– – orm	– – ibe
– – uff	– – eeze	– – eat	– – all	– – ost

c) Add one of the letters *b, f, p, s* in front of each word to produce a consonant blend at the beginning of each word. Underline the consonant blend:

– rock	– kill	– lay	– rain	– take
– kit	– lot	– right	– tar	– late
– lump	– ranch	– tack	– lock	– rag
– rake	– lace	– top	– room	– lip

d) Underline all of the beginning consonant blends in the following sentences.

1. Jane bought a *st*ory book at the *st*ore.
2. *Pl*ease, may I *pl*ay when I *cl*ean off my *pl*ate?
3. *Sm*art boys *dr*ink *fr*esh milk *fr*om the farm.
4. *Sm*itty *tr*aded his *dr*um for a book full of *st*amps.

A list of easier consonant-blend words which might be used in board- or seat-work exercises is found in Table 6 following this chapter.

SUBSTITUTION OF INITIAL CONSONANT SOUNDS

Day by day, in the early stages of reading instruction, the child is learning both *sight words* and the *sounds* of initial consonants. Knowledge thus gained can be applied in arriving at the pronunciation of other words not known as sight words. Assume the child knows the words *king* and *ring*, and meets the unknown word *sing*. He should be able to combine the *s* sound, which he knows in words like *sat, some* or *say,* with the sound of *ing* found in *king* and *ring*. This involves a process of "thinking the sounds."[1]

For illustrative purposes, let us assume that:

1. a child has learned the italicized words in Table 1,

2. he has learned the sound of the initial consonant as heard in these italicized words,

3. he has not met or learned any of the other thirty-five words in Table 1, and

4. by using his knowledge, plus some guidance from the teacher, he should be able to sound out all of the words in Table 1.

TABLE 1

bat	*can*	*fit*	*had*	*map*	*pet*	*run*	*say*
cat	ban	bit	bad	cap	bet	bun	bay
fat	fan	hit	fad	rap	met	fun	hay
hat	man	pit	mad	sap	set	sun	may
mat	pan	sit	pad				pay
pat	ran		sad				ray
rat							

---

[1] For a further discussion of this principle, see William S. Gray, *On Their Own in Reading*.

By the process of "thinking the sound" of any known consonant and blending this sound with the phonogram which concludes a known sight word, the child should be able to pronounce the new word.

1. Place a known word on the board.   bat

2. Have the children observe closely as the initial *b* is erased,   – at
and a different known consonant is substituted.   cat

3. Follow the same procedure, substituting other consonants
to make easy words.   *f*at

*h*at

*m*at

*r*at

For convenience in building mental substitution exercises, Table 7 provides a series of "word families." In each of these, the words end in a common phonogram (*et, ick, ack, ay, op, un, ill, am, ug, ed,* etc.). Not all words cited need be used in beginning reading, and those beginning with blends should not be used in substitution exercises until the sounds of these blends have been taught.

SOUNDING CONSONANTS AT END OF WORDS

The sounds of the various consonants have been taught as they occur at the beginning of words. The same procedures may be used for teaching children to *hear* these sounds at the end of words. Teaching one final consonant sound (t) is illustrated.

1. Place stimulus words on board.
2. Have children see this letter.
3. Pronounce each word carefully, so that children hear the sound at the end of the word.

4. Have children pronounce words—and supply others which end with this sound.

Stimulus words which might be used in board- or seat-work exercises:

b	d	f	g	k (ck)	l (ll)	m
Bob	sad	if	dog	back	call	him
tub	fed	calf	big	rock	tell	room
club	send	muff	flag	black	hill	gum
grab	glad	stiff	rug	trick	pull	ham
rob	cold	puff	drug	duck	still	whom
rib	band	off	bag	pick	small	drum

n	p	r	s (s)	s (=z)	t
can	hop	for	bus	his	cat
win	cap	star	yes	as	met
men	stop	her	dress	ours	shut
thin	up	dear	us	is	hit
when	step	door	less	has	set
ran	skip	clear	likes	runs	sat
moon	map	car	miss	days	but

TEACHING CONSONANT BLENDS AND DIGRAPHS AT END OF WORDS

1. The *sounds* of these letter combinations will have been taught as they occur at the beginning of words (see pp. 29-33).

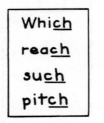

2. Procedures for teaching these sounds at the end of words may parallel those used for teaching initial sounds.

    a) Place stimulus words on board.

    b) Have children "see" the letter combinations under discussion.

c) Pronounce each word carefully so children *hear* sound at end of word.

d) Have children pronounce words.

Stimulus words, (ending with common blends and digraphs), which might be used in board- or seat-work exercises:

mar*ch*	fi*sh*	ten*th*	mus*t*	as*k*	cri*sp*
chur*ch*	ca*sh*	bo*th*	fas*t*	des*k*	gra*sp*
pea*ch*	fre*sh*	nor*th*	res*t*	bris*k*	cla*sp*
bran*ch*	ru*sh*	ba*th*	coas*t*	tas*k*	gra*sp*
dit*ch*	cra*sh*	heal*th*	mos*t*	dus*k*	wi*sp*
sear*ch*	di*sh*	pa*th*	las*t*	ris*k*	ra*sp*
bea*ch*	fla*sh*	leng*th*	bes*t*	mas*k*	
pat*ch*	wi*sh*	fif*th*	toas*t*	tus*k*	
ben*ch*	pu*sh*	clo*th*	ches*t*	flas*k*	

CONSONANT DIGRAPHS (NK, NG, CK, QU)

Teaching *nk, ng, ck* involves hearing the sound of these letter combinations at the end of words or syllables. These digraphs may be taught as follows:

NK   "The sound of NK at the end of words is the sound we hear in these words."

bank	link	junk
rank	mink	sunk
sank	pink	drunk
tank	sink	shrunk

Other words which might be used in board- or seat-work exercises include:

ink, blink, drink, think; plank, drank, spank, frank; trunk, chunk, bunk.

NG   "The sound of NG at the end of words is the sound we hear in these words."

bang	king	gong	hung
gang	ring	bong	rung
hang	wing	strong	sprung
sang	sing	song	sung

CK   "The sound of CK at the end of words is the sound we hear in these words." (ck = k)

back	pick	dock	luck
pack	kick	lock	duck
sack	sick	block	truck
crack	trick	sock	buck

QU   Consonant digraph QU:
          'The letter *q* has no sound of its own and is always followed by *u*,
          which in this case does not function as a vowel. The combination
          qu is pronounced KW—as in quick, quack (= kwik, kwak).

Other *qu* words which might be used in teaching exercises include:

queen, quart, quiet, quit, Quaker, quake, quite, quarter, quail, quarrel.

CONSONANT IRREGULARITIES

Fortunately, there is less variability in consonant sounds than in vowel
sounds. Nevertheless, a number of consonants and consonant combinations result in pronunciation irregularities which must be taught. The
majority of these would fall under one of the following headings:

   a) consonants which have more than one sound (Examples: *c* = *k* or *s*;
g = *g* or *j*; *s* = *s*, *z* or *zh*.)
   b) consonants which are not sounded (Know, light, wrap)
   c) consonant combinations with unique pronunciations (ph = f;
que = k).

The letter *g* has two sounds: the hard sound of *g* as heard in the words
go, gone, game; and the *j* sound as heard in *gem, giant, generous.* Since
the hard *g* sound occurs most frequently in words used for beginning
instruction, it is usually taught first. On the other hand, both sounds may
be taught together if it is stressed that the hard *g* sound will be met most
frequently.

The consonant *c* has two sounds. The letter *c* sounded as *k* occurs most
frequently in English words (cat, cold, cut, could, came—pronounced *kat,
kold, kut, kood, kām*). The consonant *c* is also sounded as *s* in *city, cent,
circle, center.* Eight words on the Dolch List begin with the letter *c,* and in
all of these the letter has its *k* sound. Only four of the fifty-eight words on
the Dale List, which begin with *c,* have the *s* sound. There is a phonic
principle which applies in a number of cases:

The letter *c* has the sound of *k* (cat = *k*at), except when *c* is followed by *e, i,* or *y,* in which cases, *c* usually has the sound of *s.*

The following lists of words can be used for teaching the two sounds
of the letter *c.* Note that in each of these words:

c is not followed by *e*, *i*, or *y*— the *c* is sounded as *k*			*c* is followed by *e*, *i*, or *y*—the *c* is sounded as *s*		
call	cat	cold	cent	city	circle
cup	cut	cake	cellar	place	center
came	coat	come	cider	cycle	voice
can	corn	cap	glance	cedar	citizen
could	carry	catch	cement	bicycle	mice
color	cow	care	certain	ceiling	cypress

Que at the end of words has the sound of *k;* usually *que* is blended with the preceding syllable.

picturesque	pik chure esk		plaque	plăk
antique	ăn těk		grotesque	grō̇ těsk
burlesque	bûr lěsk		clique	klēk
opaque	o pāke		brusque	brŭsk
critique	krĭ tēk		technique	tek nēk

(Note that the final syllable in *que* words is accented.)

The letter combination *ph* has the sound of *f* (photo = foto). Blackboard eye-ear exercise:

photograph = fōtȯgráf	Phillip = fĭl lĭp
alphabet = ăl fá bĕt	phonograph = fōn o grăf
Philadelphia = fĭl á dĕl fĭ á	hyphen = hī fĕn

Word list for teaching the sound of *ph*:

phone	phrase	orphan	phobia	saxophone
graph	nephew	physics	symphony	geography
photo	philosophy	asphalt	emphasize	phonics
telephone	typhoon	prophet	physical	phamphlet
autograph	phase	sophomore	sphere	biography

The letter *s* may be sounded in several ways. The most common and the most logical sound to teach is the *s* sound, as heard in "say," "sell," "sit," "some," "sunk." A single *s* sometimes has the sound of *z*: his = hiz; days = daz; as = az; runs = runz. The letter *s* is sometimes sounded *sh* as in *sure* (= shur) and *sugar* (= shugar), or *zh* as in *treasure*. The *sh* and *zh* sounds of *s* may be introduced much later than the *s* and *z* sounds.

SILENT CONSONANTS:

A number of English words contain one or more silent letters. The majority of these words are learned as sight words. Instant word recognition and independent reading are enhanced by deliberately calling to the child's attention the more frequently occurring instances of silent consonants. A number of generalizations covering silent consonants are listed below, followed by exercise material which can be used in chalkboard or seat-work exercises.

1. In words containing double consonants, only one is sounded.
2. In words beginning with *kn*, the *k* is usually silent.
3. The combination *gh* is usually silent when preceded by the vowel *i*.
4. In words beginning with *wr*, the *w* is usually silent.
5. In words ending with the syllable *ten*, the *t* is often silent.
6. In words containing *ck*, the *c* is usually silent.
7. In words ending with *mb*, the *b* is usually silent.

It is doubtful that learning the above rules in isolation or as a *series* of generalizations has virtue. Working with a series of stimulus words which follow one or more of these rules will help the child gain insight into the pronunciation of words.

TABLE 2

double consonants	*kn words*	*gh words*	*-ten ending*	*-ck ending*	*-mb ending*	*wr words*
ladder	know	sigh	often	sack	comb	write
collect	knee	light	soften	neck	thumb	wring
fellow	knight	sight	listen	block	climb	wrote
message	knew	bright	hasten	kick	bomb	wrap
roller	knit	flight	fasten	duck	lamb	wrath
summer	knife	night	glisten	clock	plumb	wrist
dinner	knock	might	moisten	black	limb	wrong
yellow	kneel	slight	brighten	trick	numb	wren
happen	knob	blight	tighten	back	crumb	wreck
kitten	known	right	frighten	pick	dumb	wreath

While a given generalization may be introduced in a particular grade, it will probably have to be reviewed in subsequent grades. For some children, simple review will not be adequate. The generalization and applications will have to be retaught. By means of close observation or diagnosis, the teacher—at any grade level—discovers which children need help on a particular skill. She can work individually with these children or devise seat-work exercises which provide practice in the areas in which they are deficient.

Table 2 contains columns of words which follow one of the previously cited rules. Words of appropriate difficulty can be selected for use in various types of teaching exercises. The difficulty level of the exercises can be further controlled by the task or tasks which the child is called upon to perform. (see Tables 2 and 3).

TABLE 3

Task I: Pronounce all the words in each *A* column.

Task II: Strike out each silent consonant in the words in the *A* columns (the first one is done for you).

Task III: In the *B* columns, write the dictionary pronunciation of each word.

A	B	A	B
si~~gh~~t	sit	knight	
hasten		glisten	
knew		comb	
rabbit		right	
thick		write	
climb		black	
wrote		funnel	
dollar		known	
debt		doubt	
knock		truck	
soften		often	
summer		tunnel	
sigh		thumb	
wrap		knelt	
knob		listen	

The following exercise illustrates that silent letters are useful in that they produce a different word which has the same pronunciation but a different meaning from the word to which the silent letter is added. The silent letter provides a VISUAL clue to the meaning of the new word.

TABLE 4

In column *B*, add a silent letter or letters to each word in column *A* in order to produce a different word.

A	B	A	B
new	_____	rest	_____
hole	_____	be	_____
our	_____	cent	_____
rap	_____	not	_____
nob	_____	plum	_____
in	_____	no	_____
night	_____	to	_____
ring	_____	so	_____

TEACHING CONTRACTIONS

Contractions result from major structural changes in words and should be taught as sight words. Two illustrative teaching and testing exercises are presented. In exercise *A*, the child selects the proper contractions from a list provided; in exercise *B*, he must *supply* the correct form from memory.

Contractions are single words formed by combining two words but omitting a letter or letters. An apostrophe (') is always inserted where a letter or letters have been omitted.

A. Write the contraction for each of the pairs of words below. The contractions you will need to use are included on the next line:

he'll, I'll, didn't, they've, haven't, isn't, musn't, I'm

1. did not _____   5. is not _____
2. he will _____   6. they have _____
3. have not _____   7. I will _____
4. must not _____   8. I am _____

B. Write the contractions for each of the pairs of words below. Remember an apostrophe is part of the spelling.

1. is not _____	4. should not _____
2. I am _____	5. they have _____
3. they are _____	6. you are _____

List of contractions for use in board- or seat-work exercises:

can't, they've, I'll, it's, there's, wouldn't, doesn't, hadn't, you're, hasn't, I've, don't, she'll, shouldn't, they'd, musn't, he'll, isn't, didn't, you're, she's, I'm, wasn't, haven't, they're, he's, couldn't.

SUMMARY OF PHONIC GENERALIZATIONS

1. Consonants
   a) Consonant sounds are consistent; a large majority of consonants have one "regular" sound which is quite consistent in English words. The consonants which meet this description are *b, d, f, h, j, k, l, m, n, p, r, t, v, w*, and initial *y*.
2. Consonants which combine
   a) *Consonant blends* are two or more letters which are blended so that sound elements of each letter are heard—*bl, bl*ack; *str, str*ing; *spl, spl*ash; *gl, gl*ide.
   b) *Consonant digraphs* are two-letter combinations which result in one speech sound that is not a blend of the letters involved —*sh*all; *wh*ite; *th*is (voiced *th*); *th*ink (unvoiced *th*); *ch*air, *ch*orus (ch = k); chef (ch = sh).
3. Irregular spellings
   a) Silent consonants in specific combinations
      1) The *k* is silent in *kn* (knew, knee).
      2) Double consonants—only one is sounded (sum*m*er).
      3) When vowel *i* precedes *gh*, the latter is silent (li*gh*t).
      4) The *w* is silent in *wr* at the beginning of words (*w*ring).
      5) When *t* follows *s* or *f*, the *t* is sometimes silent (of*t*en, fas*t*en).
      6) In *ck* combinations, *c* is silent (sa*c*k, clo*c*k).
      7) The *b* is silent in *mb* at the end of words (com*b*, lam*b*).
4. Two sounds for consonant *c*
   a) *c* = *k* in *cake, corn, curl*.
   b) *c* = *s* when followed by *i, e, y* (city, cent, cycle).

5. Two sounds for consonant *g*
   a) regular sound in *go, game, gum.*
   b) *g = j* when followed by *e, i* (gem, giant).
6. *Ph = f* (photo = foto; graph = graf).
7. *Qu = kw* (quack = kwack). The letter *q* has no sound of its own. In English spellings, *q* is always followed by the letter *u.*
8. The letter *s* may be sounded in a number of ways.
   a) *s = s* (most common) (sell, soft, said).
   b) *s = z* (his = hiz; runs = runz).
   c) *s = sh, zh* (sugar, treasure).

SUMMARY

This chapter opened with a discussion of the prerequisites a child needs in order to profit from phonics instruction. The learner must be able to:

1. make auditory discrimination between similar speech sounds
2. distinguish visually between letters and words.

When these abilities have not been developed, there is no basis for teaching phonic analysis. The teaching of these skills is usually stressed in what has come to be labeled the "reading-readiness program." It is essential that these important skills be seen as part of the systematic instructional program.

Once the child has acquired adequate auditory and visual discrimination skills, he is ready for instruction in associating the speech sound of letters, syllables, etc. with the printed symbols. The balance of Chapter 2 provided illustrations of teaching procedures. It should be kept in mind that the intent was to present illustrative examples, rather than to prescribe. Tables 5, 6, and 7, which follow, are compilations of words which might be used in teaching particular phonic skills.

TABLE 5

A list of easier words for use in board- or seat-work exercises in teaching initial sound of consonants

c = k	d	f	hard g	h	j	k	l
can	did	fast	go	hat	jump	keep	let
cap	do	far	game	hand	just	kind	like
car	done	feel	gate	hill	Jane	king	love
cold	down	fall	garden	hair	Jack	kept	lady
carry	deep	first	gave	his	joy	key	light
cow	dinner	fun	gift	hold	jam	kick	look
cry	day	full	give	head	jar	kill	lake
cut	dear	father	get	hot	jelly	kiss	little
come	dark	farm	gold	have	jet	kite	last
cup	dish	face	got	he	job	kitten	listen
cat	damp	fly	gone	him	joke	Kate	letter
cake	deed	for	good	had	June	kettle	late
coat	dip	found	gain	how	join	keg	lost

m	n	p	r	s	t	v	w
most	new	pan	red	see	tell	very	walk
man	not	pass	rain	sit	ten	visit	wash
my	near	put	rest	some	to	voice	want
must	need	pull	ran	save	talk	valley	word
may	nice	paid	room	sing	took	view	wish
me	night	party	ride	say	told	velvet	work
much	noon	people	road	same	take	vote	wait
many	name	pick	run	soon	tall		window
meet	no	paper	right	sat	time	y	will
milk	none	paint	real	seen	too	yes	went
made	now	pen	river	set	table	you	wall
meat	never	part	race	so	top	yard	warm
mine	north	person	rat	soft	tail	yet	win
move	next	pig	ring	said	tap	your	water
men	nap	pork	roll	soap	tent	yellow	winter

45

TABLE 6

A list of words for use in board- or seat-work exercises for teaching initial consonant blends

br	cr	dr	fr	gr	pr	tr
brother	cry	dress	friend	grade	pretty	tree
bring	cross	drink	from	great	present	train
brought	crop	draw	front	ground	president	trip
brown	creek	dry	Friday	green	program	truly
brake	crowd	drive	fruit	grandmother	print	trick
bread	cream	drop	fright	grass	produce	truck
bright	crack	dream	free	grandfather	prize	trade
bridge	crawl	drove	fresh	group	promise	trap
break	crib	drum	frog	grew	proud	track
brave	cried	drew	freeze	gray	product	true
brush	crumb	drill	frozen	grain	prepare	trail
branch	crown	drag	friendly	grab	protect	treat
brick	crow	drank	fry	grape	press	trim
broom	crook	drug	frost	grand	price	tramp

bl	cl	fl	pl	sl	sp	st
black	close	flower	play	sleep	spell	start
blue	clean	fly	place	sled	spend	stay
blow	class	floor	please	slid	spot	story
block	clothes	flag	plant	slate	speak	stop
bloom	climb	flew	plan	slip	spent	store
blew	club	flood	plane	slowly	sport	study
blanket	cloth	float	plenty	slave	speed	still
blood	cloud	flat	plain	slow	spoke	state
blackboard	clear	flour	plate	slipper	spirit	stand
blossom	clay		pleasant	slept	speech	stick
blind	clothing	gl	plow	sleet	spoon	stocking
blame	clock	glad	player	sleepy	spear	step
blizzard	climate	glass	plantation	slim	space	star
blaze	clown	glove	playmate	slick	spin	stood

46

Table 6 (Cont.)

sm	sn	sc	sk	sw	tw
small	snow	school	skate	swim	twelve
smoke	snake	scare	skin	sweet	twist
smell	snowball	scold	sky	swing	twenty
smile	snail	scout	ski	sweater	twice
smart	snap	scream	skip	swan	twin
smooth	snug	schoolhouse	skirt	sweep	twig
smack	sneeze	score	skunk	swell	twinkle

TABLE 7

A list of easier words for use in board- or seat-work exercises in teaching substitution of initial consonant sounds. Each series contains "family words" or words which end with a common phonogram. It will also be noted that some of these phonograms are little words—*at, an, it,* etc. However, in every case we are dealing with the *sound* that occurs at the end of a word, not with sounding little words in larger words.

back	bake	day	cap	bug	bank	cot	Dick
Jack	cake	gay	gap	dug	rank	dot	kick
lack	fake	hay	lap	hug	sank	got	lick
pack	lake	lay	map	jug	tank	hot	nick
rack	make	may	nap	mug	(blank)	lot	pick
sack	rake	pay	rap	rug	(crank)	not	sick
tack	sake	ray	tap	tug	(drank)	pot	(brick)
(black)	take	say	(clap)	(chug)	(flank)	(blot)	(chick)
(crack)	wake	way	(flap)	(drug)	(frank)	(plot)	(slick)
(shack)	(brake)	(clay)	(slap)	(plug)	(plank)	(shot)	(stick)
(slack)	(flake)	(play)	(snap)	(slug)	(prank)	(slot)	(thick)
(stack)	(shake)	(stray)	(strap)	(smug)	(spank)	(spot)	(trick)
(track)	(snake)	(tray)	(trap)	(snug)	(thank)	(trot)	(click)

bag	bail	gain	bat	bump	can	came	Bill
gag	fail	lain	cat	dump	Dan	dame	fill
lag	hail	main	fat	hump	fan	fame	hill
nag	mail	pain	hat	jump	man	game	kill
rag	nail	rain	mat	lump	pan	lame	mill
sag	pail	vain	pat	pump	ran	name	pill
tag	rail	(brain)	rat	(chump)	tan	same	will
wag	sail	(drain)	sat	(plump)	van	tame	(drill)
(brag)	tail	(grain)	(brat)	(slump)	(bran)	(blame)	(skill)
(drag)	(frail)	(plain)	(flat)	(stump)	(clan)	(flame)	(spill)
(flag)	(trail)	(train)	(scat)	(thump)	(plan)	(frame)	(still)
(snag)	(snail)						

Table 7 (Cont.)

best	bet	bunk	bell	bit	dim	dear	bad
lest	get	dunk	fell	fit	him	fear	dad
jest	jet	hunk	sell	hit	Jim	hear	fad
pest	let	junk	tell	pit	rim	near	had
rest	met	sunk	well	sit	Tim	rear	lad
test	net	(drunk)	yell	wit	(brim)	tear	mad
vest	pet	(flunk)	(shell)	(flit)	(grim)	year	pad
zest	set	(skunk)	(smell)	(grit)	(slim)	(clear)	sad
(blest)	wet	(spunk)	(spell)	(slit)	(swim)	(smear)	(glad)
(crest)	(fret)	(trunk)	(swell)	(split)	(trim)	(spear)	

bold	hop	bed	buck	band	beat	bend	ball	bun
cold	mop	fed	duck	hand	heat	lend	call	fun
fold	pop	led	luck	land	meat	mend	fall	gun
gold	top	Ned	suck	sand	neat	send	hall	run
hold	(crop)	red	tuck	(brand)	seat	tend	tall	sun
mold	(drop)	Ted	(pluck)	(gland)	(cheat)	(blend)	wall	(spun)
sold	(flop)	(bled)	(struck)	(grand)	(treat)	(spend)	(small)	(stun)
told	(shop)	(fled)	(stuck)	(stand)	(wheat)		(stall)	
(scold)	(stop)	(sled)	(truck)					

Chapter 3

Teaching Vowel Sounds

Teaching vowel sounds is undoubtedly the most difficult part of phonics instruction. This is true primarily because of the great variability in sound that a vowel or vowel combination may have in different words. Some of these differences are quite minute, and being unable to distinguish between them would not seriously handicap a person in learning to read—assuming, of course, that he can pronounce the words in question. For instance, the differences in the sound of the vowel *a* in *loyal, almost, idea, path, father* are not likely to pose a problem in beginning reading. To profit from phonics instruction, one must be able to discriminate between such vowel sounds as are heard in the words *pin, pen, pan, pun; apple, able; book, boot; not, note;* and the like.

In teaching phonic analysis, deciding which vowel, or which sound of that vowel, to teach first is probably not a crucial issue. The reasons usually advanced for teaching the short sounds first are these:

1. A majority of the words a child meets in beginning reading contain short vowel sounds.

2. Many of these words are single-vowel-in-medial-position words. The phonic generalization covering this situation is one that holds or applies in a large percentage of words met in beginning reading: One vowel in the middle of a word (or syllable) usually has its short sound.

Advocacy of teaching long vowel sounds first rests on the fact that the vowel name *is* the long sound of the vowel (A E I O U). This is an easy sound to master.

It should be recalled that one of the virtues of teaching some sight-recognition words before starting on phonic analysis is that the sight words learned can then serve as "phonic models." In this approach children work with sounds as heard in words, not sounds assigned to letters in isolation. This latter practice was one of the major weaknesses of earlier phonics instruction. Children worked with sounds of letters divorced from how the letters sounded in KNOWN words:

C was pronounced *kuh*; *A* = *ah*; *T* = *tuh*: *kuh at tuh* = *cat.*

As one begins the teaching of vowel sounds, it is important to keep in mind what learnings have taken place prior to this activity:

1. The child understands and uses spoken language.
2. The school has provided extended practice on auditory-visual discrimination.
3. Children have learned a number of SIGHT words.
4. Sounds of consonants have been learned:
   m sounds as heard in *man, milk, mop*
   c sounds as heard in *cat (kat), cake*
   t sounds as heard in *take, toy*—and other consonant sounds.

There are two approaches to teaching the short sound of vowels in words of one syllable. One of these is to deal separately with single initial and medial vowels. The other combines the teaching of these two vowel situations. The generalizations on which either approach is based are:

1. A single vowel in medial position usually has its short sound.
2. A single vowel which does not conclude a word usually has its short sound.

In the material which follows, the short sounds of the vowels in medial position are taught first—followed by an illustration of teaching single initial and single medial vowels together.

TEACHING SHORT *A* SOUND

The teacher may say, "We have learned the sounds that consonants make in words. You can hear the sound of *b* in *bat, d* in *dad, m* in *man.*

Now we are going to learn to hear the sounds that vowels make in words. The vowel letters in our alphabet are: A a—E e—I i—O o—U u. [Pronounce each vowel as it is written on the chalkboard.] Let's all say these letters together—ready, A—E—I—O—U. When we say the name of the vowel letter, we hear what is called the vowel's long sound.

Today we are going to listen carefully and learn to hear another sound for the vowel *a*—its short sound. I am going to put some words on the board. We have studied these words before. Each of the words has the letter *a* in it. Listen to the sound the *a* has in each word.

cat
stand
man
ham
cap
back

1. Pronounce each word, moving hand from left to right through the word.

2. Emphasize the sound of *a* (*ah*), but do not detach the sound.

3. Have the children say the words in unison, asking them to listen for the sound of ă.

4. Stress that the sound heard is called the short sound of *a*. Have the children note how this sound differs from the letter name.

5. Ask pupils how many vowels they see in each word and where the vowel is located (middle of word).

6. Have children state what sound is heard when there is one vowel in the middle of a word.

7. Have children state, in their own words, the rule which covers this vowel situation.[1]

---

[1] From the standpoint of the teacher, the generalizations which apply to vowel situations do not qualify as "rules." However, in teaching children, these generalizations are called rules and each is qualified by the term "usually."

Using this approach the generalization will evolve: One vowel in the middle of the word usually has its short sound. (It is probably not essential that each child be able to recite all of the generalizations discussed in this chapter.) At this point, it might be profitable to cite other familiar words which follow the generalizations under discussion, even though all the stimulus words used are not yet known as sight words.

A	B
ran	răn
bat	băt
Sam	Săm
bag	băg
bank	bănk
trap	trăp
glad	glăd
hat	hăt

1. Place on the board other words, all of which have the single vowel *a* in medial position.

2. Have children note short sound of *a*. (If the teacher wishes, she may mark the vowels *ă*, explaining this mark [˘] may be used to indicate the short vowel sound.)
(See column *B*).

Below are a number of words which have the medial short *a* sound. These are usually met in beginning or early primary level reading.

bad	camp	fact	hat	match	stand
back	cat	flag	hang	plan	shall
bat	clap	flat	Jack	pal	sack
band	catch	flash	lamp	pan	sank
bang	dad	grand	land	pat	sang
bank	dash	grab	lad	quack	tan
black	drag	hand	man	rag	track
cap	fan	had	map	ranch	thank
can	fat	ham	mad	sad	

SHORT SOUND OF *I*

REVIEW

1. "Who can name the vowels?"
2. "What vowel did we study last?"
3. "Today we will listen for the short sound of the vowel *i*. Remember, the short sound of vowels is marked ˘. I am going to put some words on the board—words we already know. All the words will have the vowel *i* in them. Listen and hear how the *i* is sounded when we pronounce the words."

STEPS

1. Teacher pronounces each word.
2. Children (in unison) pronounce each word.

3. Children note:
    a) Each word contains the vowel *i*.
    b) *I* is in the middle of the word.
    c) *I* has its short sound.
4. Call for rule previously learned: One vowel in the middle of a word (usually) has the short sound.
5. Have children volunteer other words with medial short *i* to be listed on board.

VARIATION: USE OF WORD FAMILIES

Some teachers find that certain children can do better in "fixing" the short sound of a given vowel if they see and pronounce a series of words which contain larger identical units than the vowel alone: the words *big, ship, tin, hill* have an identical unit—*i*. The words *big, pig, dig, fig;* or *hill, fill, bill, pill;* or *sit, fit, bit, kit* have rhyming units composed of several letters which have precisely the same phonic value in each word. Word families could be used both for teaching common phonic elements and for rapid recognition as sight words.

Below are a number of words containing the medial short *i* sound. These words are usually met in beginning or early primary-level reading.

big	Dick	fit	lift	slip	skin	did
dig	brick	bit	gift	trip	chin	lid
pig	pick	sit	drift	skip	thing	hid
fig	kick	pit	swift	drip	ring	pitch
tin	sick	kit	dish	ship	king	rich
fin	stick	him	fish	tip	sing	will
win	thick	rim	wish	rip	swing	hill
pin	silk	swim	skirt	miss	bring	still
sin	milk	skim	dirt	kiss	spring	mill

TEACHING THE SHORT SOUND OF *E*

1. Review concepts previously introduced.
   a) Have pupils name the vowels.
   b) Tell what vowel sounds have been studied previously.
   c) State the rule learned: One vowel in the middle of a word usually has its short sound.

A	B
bet	pen
get	dress
pet	let
let	bell
set	red

2. Put short-*e* stimulus words on board.

3. Column *A* illustrates word-family endings, column *B* mixed endings.

4. Teacher pronounces words.

5. Pupils say words—listening to sound of *e*.

6. Reiterate rule learned previously (see Item 1*c* above).

7. Have children cite other words.

8. Reinforce learning with seat-work exercises. (Make sure child does not rely on *visual cues* alone.)

9. Teacher works with small groups or with individual children who have not mastered concepts and sound taught thus far.

Words containing short *e* sound (medial position) which can be used in board work or in preparing seat-work exercises:

led	net	get	yes	self	less
red	bet	held	west	kept	spell
fed	pet	rest	step	fell	when
bed	yet	dress	bend	sell	fresh
leg	let	men	went	tell	well
help	wet	ten	send	well	sent
set	met	pen	tent	smell	sled

SHORT SOUND OF *U*

Follow steps outlined previously for teaching short vowel sounds.

1. "Who will name the vowels?"

2. Ask the children what vowel sounds have been studied.

3. Have pupils say the rule learned previously: One vowel in the middle of a word usually has its short sound.

A	B
bug	bus
hug	tub
dug	pup
rug	jump
jug	much

4. Put short-*u* stimulus words on board.

5. Column *A* illustrates word-family endings, column *B* mixed endings.

6. Teacher pronounces words.

7. Pupils say words—listening to sound of *u*.

8. Children note that rule learned previously applies here (see Item 3 above).

9. Children give other words (short *u* sound in medial position). These can be added to lists on the board.

10. Reinforce learning with seat-work exercises. (Make sure child does not rely on visual cues alone.)

11. Teacher works with small groups or with individual children who have not mastered sounds and concepts taught thus far.

12. Review words having short *a*, *i*, or *e* sound.

Words containing short *u* sound (medial position) which can be used in board work or in preparing seat-work exercises:

gun	rub	bump	duck	sunk	jug
run	tub	dump	luck	chum	rug
fun	club	jump	truck	fuss	dug
sun	must	gum	suck	dull	bug
bun	trust	hum	hung	but	drum
cup	bust	sum	sung	cut	bud
shut	dust	puff	rung	hut	stub

SHORT SOUND OF *O*

Follow steps outlined previously in teaching short vowel sounds (*a, i, e, u,* above).

1. "Who will name the vowels?"

2. "What vowel sounds have we studied?"

3. "Who can say the rule we have learned?" One vowel in middle of word (or syllable) usually has its short sound.

4. Put short-*o* stimulus words on board.

5. Column *A*—word-family endings, column *B*—mixed endings.

6. Teacher pronounces these words.

7. Children note single vowel in middle of word.

8. Pupils say words—listening to the sound of *o*.

```
┌─────────────────────────┐
│   A        B            │
│  got     shot           │
│  hot     rock           │
│  lot     doll           │
│  not     box            │
│  pot     drop           │
│                         │
└─────────────────────────┘
```

9. Children give other words (short *o* in medial position). These can be added to words on board.

10. Reinforce learning with seat-work exercises.

Words containing short *o* sound (medial position) which can be used in board work or in preparing seat-work exercises:

stop	job	shot	sock	chop	pond
drop	rob	not	fox	blot	frog
mop	Bob	shop	clock	mop	lock
hop	sob	doll	block	hop	nod
pop	cob	dock	top	cot	bond
crop	pond	rock	from	lot	trot

TEACHING SHORT SOUND OF INITIAL AND MEDIAL VOWELS AS ONE GENERALIZATION

Some teachers prefer to teach the short sound of *initial* and *medial* vowels simultaneously. The procedure can be much the same as discussed above for the medial-vowel situation. However, the generalization which emerges will be stated differently. To illustrate this concept, place a number of stimulus words on the board.

Words in column *A* contain one vowel (initial), and the short sound is heard. Words in column *B* contain one vowel (medial), and the short vowel is heard. As the children see and hear these characteristics, the following generalization will emerge:

When there is one vowel in a word and the vowel does not come at the end of the word, it has its short sound.

```
┌─────────────┐  ┌─────────────┐
│      A      │  │      B      │
│     act     │  │     hat     │
│     am      │  │     ran     │
│     as      │  │    shall    │
│     at      │  │    hand     │
│     ask     │  │     man     │
└─────────────┘  └─────────────┘
```

THE SCHWA SOUND

In a large number of words of more than one syllable, there is a diminished stress on one of the syllables. The sound of the vowel in these unstressed syllables undergoes a slight change which is referred to as "a softening of the vowel sound." This softened vowel sound is called the *schwa* sound, and is represented by the symbol ə.

All of the vowels are represented by the schwa sound as illustrated by each of the italicized vowels in the following words.

$$
\begin{aligned}
\text{bedl}a\text{m} &= \text{bed}' \text{ ləm} \\
\text{beat}e\text{n} &= \text{bēt}' \text{ ən} \\
\text{beaut}i\text{ful} &= \text{bū}' \text{ tə fəl} \\
\text{beck}o\text{n} &= \text{bek}' \text{ ən}
\end{aligned}
$$

In other words, if vowels were interchanged in unstressed syllables, the spellings would change but the sound heard would remain the same for the different vowels. For instance, read both of the following sentences without stressing the second syllable in any word.

A. "Button, button, who has the button?"
B. "Buttun, buttan, who has the butten?"

If, in reading sentence *B* you give each second syllable the same stress as was given in the word directly above it, the sounds remain constant. Thus, teaching the schwa sound in the initial stages of reading would have little impact on one's ability to sound out words. However, once the child begins to use a dictionary which utilizes the schwa symbol, ə, the points discussed above would have to be explained.

LONG VOWEL SOUNDS

In teaching the long sounds of vowels, the following principles should be kept in mind.

1. The primary objective is not to teach rules, but rather to teach in such a way that the child sees the application. The phonic generalization should emerge from the words being studied.

2. The learner should not be overburdened with generalizations which have limited application in learning to read. If a generalization applies to only two or three words that a child will meet in beginning reading, teach these words as sight words.

3. Work first with those rules or generalizations which hold or apply in a wide number of cases.

4. Teach non-phonetic spellings as sight words.

Below, several generalizations are listed, followed by brief illustrations for teaching. Some teachers prefer to teach each generalization separately, others prefer to combine two or more.

1. When there are two vowels together, the first usually has its long sound; the second is silent (feed, boat, seat, rain = f ē ȩ́d, b ō ȧ́t, s ē ȧ́t, r ā ẏ́n).

2. In words with two vowels, one of which is final *e*, the *e* is silent and the first vowel is usually long. (take = t ā k ȩ́; bone = b ō n ȩ́; tube = t ū b ȩ́.)

3. The combination *ay* at the end of a word has the sound of long *a*. (NOTE: Generalizations 1, 2, and 3 can be combined to read: "When a word contains two vowels, the first is usually long and the second is silent." This will include all instances where the final-*e* rule holds. However, the final-*e* rule is one of the easiest for children to grasp. Many teachers consider this ample justification for teaching it separately. Also, the more inclusive statement involves the understanding that *y* at the end of a word functions as a vowel.)

4. When the only vowel in a word comes at the end of the word, it usually has its long sound (go, me, by). (NOTE: Sometimes the *y* generalization is taught separately. "In a word ending in *y*, and having no other vowel, the *y* has the long sound of *i*.")

TEACHING THE GENERALIZATION INVOLVING TWO ADJACENT VOWELS

(Two vowels together—the first usually has its long sound and the second is silent.) In the illustrations which follow, teaching does not start with a statement of the generalization, but with material which will help children discover the generalization. The two-vowel generalization holds fairly consistently for *ee, oa, ai, ea,* and does *not* apply equally well for *au, ou, ui, eu.*[2]

One way to illustrate and teach this generalization is to place on the board four columns of words. Each column should consist of words which contain one of the vowel combinations *oa, ai, ea,* or *ee.*

<u>1</u>	<u>2</u>	<u>3</u>	<u>4</u>
boat	chain	beat	feed
coat	mail	dream	seed
load	wait	leaf	keep
road	rain	teach	queen
soak	paid	seat	steel

1. Pronounce each word in the first column. "Do you hear the $\bar{o}$ sound? Does the vowel say its name?"

2. Children read words in Column 1 and listen to the sound of $\bar{o}$.

3. Pronounce the words in Column 2. "What vowel sound do you hear? ($\bar{a}$) What vowels do you see?" (ai)

4. Do the same for words in each column. Point out that in each word, you *hear* the long sound of the first vowel and that the second vowel is not sounded.

boat = b ō a̸ t = bōt	beat = b ē a̸ t = bēt
rain = r ā i̸ n = rān	feed = f ē e̸ d = fēd

---

[2] For a discussion of how consistently these rules apply, see Alvina Treut Burrows and Zyra Lourie, "Two Vowels Go Walking," *The Reading Teacher,* XVII, November 1963; and Theodore Clymer, "The Utility of Phonic Generalizations in the Primary Grades," *The Reading Teacher,* XVI, January 1963; Ruth Oaks, "A Study of the Vowel Situations in a Primary Vocabulary," *Education,* LXXII, May 1952.

A	B	C
set	se t	seat
cot	co t	coat
men	me n	mean
fed	fe d	feed
got	go t	goat
pan	pa n	pain
man	ma n	main
bet	be t	beat

A second illustration is to place a column of single-medial vowels on the board (column *A*). Have children note that they hear the short vowel sound. Then, write words in column *B*, leaving a vacant letter space following each vowel. Add second vowel as found in words in column *C*. In each case, a different word is built in which the first vowel has its long sound and the second is silent. Other word combinations include: met—meet—meat; lad—laid; mad—maid; plan—plain; bed—bead; net—neat; step—steep.

Below are a number of *oa, ai, ea,* and *ee* words which may be used in board-work or seat-work exercises.

oa		*ai*		*ea*		*ee*	
boat	roam	rain	maid	eat	reach	deep	week
goat	coach	mail	grain	bead	clean	street	feel
soap	boast	gain	laid	bean	cream	meet	queen
coat	goal	sail	trail	deal	meal	feed	wheel
coal	coast	pain	plain	clean	meat	keep	speed
roast	groan	fail	train	steal	speak	seen	feed
float	foam	paid	tail	leak	mean	sleep	sheep
soak	toast	nail	chain	beach	dream	need	green

TEACHING THE GENERALIZATION INVOLVING FINAL E

(In two-vowel words the final *e* is silent and the previous vowel usually has its long sound.)

1. Place on the board a column of words which have a single vowel in medial position. Choose words to which a final *e* may be added to form a new word and illustrate this generalization (see column *A*).

2. Pupils pronounce words in column *A*.

3. Cite previously learned rule (single vowel in medial position usually has short sound).

4. Add final *e* to each word (as in column *B*).

5. Pupils pronounce words in column *B* and listen to vowel sound heard.

6. Ask children for generalization (the final *e* is silent and the first vowel is long).

7. If desired, diacritical marks may be used in column *C*.

A	**B**	**C**
hat	hate	hāte̸
hid	hide	hīd̸
past	paste	pāste̸
pal	pale	pāl̸
cut	cute	cūt̸
plan	plane	plān̸
rat	rate	rāt̸
pin	pine	pīn̸
strip	stripe	strīp̸
ride	ride	rīd̸

Other words which can be used in board-work or seat-work lessons include: fat, bath, rip, tap, twin, mat, quit, fin, win, cap, bit, dim, can, kit, pan, etc.

TEACHING GENERALIZATION OF SINGLE-FINAL VOWEL

(When the only vowel in a word comes at the end of the word, it has its long sound.) In general, this statement also applies to single vowels which conclude accented syllables.

1. Place on the board words that contain one vowel in final position.

2. Review fact that *y* at the end of a word functions as a vowel (*y* = long *i*).

3. Teacher and pupils pronounce each word.

4. "What do you SEE that is the same in each of these words?" (They all end with one vowel.)

5. "What do you HEAR in each of these words?" (The long vowel sound.)

6. "Could we make up a rule to fit all of these words?" (Children will say the rule in their own words and the teacher restates and writes rule on the board.)

he	go	by	try
she	no	my	fly
we	so	cry	sky
me		dry	why
be		fry	shy

TEACHING THE GENERALIZATION COVERING AY

(*Ay* at the end of words has the sound of long *a*.)

1. Children have learned: The vowels are *a–e–i–o–u* and sometimes *y*. *y* functions as a vowel in these situations:

    a) when it concludes a word which has no other vowel

    b) when it concludes words of more than one syllable (e.g., *happy*)

    c) when it immediately follows another vowel.

2. In the combination *ay*, *y* serves as a vowel (two vowels together—the second is silent, the first long).

day
may
stay
say
clay

3. Place stimulus words on board.
4. Teacher and pupils pronounce words.
5. Vowel sound heard—long sound of *a*.

Other illustrations: gay, lay, hay, play, stray, tray, away, pray, gray pay, ray, jay, may, fay, sway, spray.

SOUND OF Y AT END OF LONGER WORDS

When *y* concludes a word of two or more syllables, it has the sound heard in: hob *by*, win *dy*, fog *gy*, luc *ky*, jol *ly*, fun *ny*, hap *py*, mer *ry*, noi *sy*, rus *ty*, buz *zy*.

Most dictionaries mark this sound of *y* as short *i* (ĭ—hur ĭ, luck ĭ, etc.). However, many authorities feel that the final sound heard in the above words is closer to long *e* (ē).[3] The writer agrees with the latter position, but each teacher will have to decide this issue for herself.

Other words which might be used in teaching exercises: badly, angry, plenty, cooky, honestly, closely, beauty, mainly, guilty, history, lively, nasty, January, partly, ready, seventy, rocky, penny, muddy, simply, sorry, jelly, nearly, costly, sleepy.

TEACHING LONG AND SHORT SOUNDS TOGETHER

The sequence in which vowel sounds are taught is probably not crucial. The rationale for teaching long sounds first and that for teaching short sounds first has been reviewed previously. (See pp. 50-51.) Some teachers prefer to present both long and short sounds together in order to help the child hear the difference. Immediately following this approach, one or the other sound may be worked with extensively.

The following procedure might be used for contrasting the long and short sounds of the same vowel. The illustration will deal with only one vowel—*a*.

1. "Today we want to see if we can hear the difference between two sounds that the vowel *A* makes."

---

[3] See Leonard Bloomfield and Clarence L. Barnhart, *Let's Read* (Detroit: Wayne State University Press, 1961), p. 210; and Dolores Durkin, *Phonics and the Teaching of Reading* (No. 22, Bureau of Publications, Teachers College, Columbia University [New York, 1962]), p. 63.

```
          A - a
      I            II
    rain         ran
    main         man
    paid         pad
    maid         mad
    pail         pal
    pain         pan
```

2. Place upper- and lower-case letter on board.
3. Place long-vowel words on board (Column I).
4. Pronounce each word for children.
   a) "Do you hear the sound *a*?
   b) "Do you hear the letter's name?
   c) "When you hear the letter's name, that is its long sound—*a*."
5. Have the pupils note:
   a) Each of these words has two vowels.
   b) The first "says its name" (i.e., long sound).
   c) The second is silent.
6. Next add the words in Column II.
   a) Pronounce each word.
   b) Contrast vowel sounds heard in *rain, ran*, etc.
7. Have pupils note:
   a) Each of these words has one vowel.
   b) The vowel is in the middle of the word.
   c) The short sound of the vowel is heard.

EXAMPLES OF EXERCISES FOR
TEACHING VOWEL SOUNDS

A. Do you have a "good ear" for vowel sounds? In this exercise each vowel you see is one of the following:

1. not sounded (Use this mark /; seéd.)
2. short (Use this mark ⌣; ĭt.)
3. long (Use this mark ‗; sēéd.)

Say each word—listen to the sound you hear. Then mark each vowel using one of the above marks. (The diacritical marks are included for the teacher's ease in scoring.)

a	*e*	*i*	*o*	*u*
1. bănd	crēạm	pĭg	clŏck	cūtẹ
2. pālẹ	spĕll	hĭll	gō	bŭnch
3. grāịn	kēẹp	bītẹ	cōạl	dŭll
4. thănk	drĕss	shĭp	flōạt	fūsẹ
5. māịl	bēạch	twīng	shŏt	trŭck
6. rātẹ	strēẹt	skĭn	stōlẹ	mŭst

B. The above exercise can be made more difficult by omitting the vowel heading for each column and mixing vowel sounds within columns.

EXCEPTIONS TO VOWEL RULES PREVIOUSLY TAUGHT

There is no vowel rule or generalization which will apply in all situations. When exceptions to a given rule occur, they may be taught as sight words or a new rule can be devised to cover the exception. It has been suggested that children not be burdened with rules that have very limited applications. Different teachers will, of course, arrive at different conclusions as to which generalizations should be included in phonic instruction. Some exceptions to a given rule occur with such frequency as to merit calling the child's attention to the exceptions.

For instance, one of the most useful phonic generalizations discussed earlier states: "One vowel in medial position usually has its short sound." There follow several series of words which meet the criterion of "one vowel in medial position" but in which the vowel has its long sound.

The vowel o followed by ld usually has the long sound

old	hold	sold
mold	told	cold
gold	fold	bold

The vowel i followed by nd, gh, or ld frequently has the long sound.

find	light	wild
blind	fight	mild
behind	sight	child
mind	right	
kind		

VOWEL SOUNDS AFFECTED BY *R*

A vowel (or vowels) followed by the letter *r* results in a blended sound which is neither the short nor long sound of the vowel.

It is doubtful that this phonic fact—as it relates to learning to read —is of paramount importance. However, calling the child's attention to this role of the letter *r* is a justifiable procedure. Since the child uses and understands hundreds of words which include a vowel followed by *r*, this is not a particularly difficult fact to teach. More important, the child will have mastered several such words as sight words—these can serve as examples when the generalization is introduced.

Some of the more common "vowel *-r*" words which may be used in board-work or seat-work exercises are listed below.

-ar		*-er*	*-or*
car	yard	her	for
farm	park	person	corn
march	card	term	storm
part	far	serve	horn
star	smart	ever	short
dark	arm	certain	north
hard	bark	berth	horse
barn	tar	herd	corner
start	spark	under	form

The spelling *ir* is usually pronounced *ûr* (bird = bûrd), except when followed by a final *e* (fire) :

bird	dirt	firm	third	fir	thirst
girl	first	sir	shirt	birth	stir

a = *aw* when it is followed by *l, ll, w, u*:

talk	all	wall	saw	claw	haul
walk	tall	fall	draw	straw	because
salt	small	call	lawn	dawn	fault
halt	hall	ball	drawn	jaw	Paul

THE *OO* SOUNDS

Explaining the sounds of *oo* is much more complicated than actually learning to pronounce the frequently used words which contain this letter combination. Most words containing *oo* are pronounced in one of two ways. These sounds are designated ōō (long sound) and ŏŏ (short sound). In order to be meaningful, they must be associated with something the child knows. His speaking and listening vocabulary includes some words which have the short sound and some which have the long sound. The child needs practice in hearing the differences in these sounds.

This may be accomplished by pronouncing and discriminating between these sounds in known words.

> "The bōōt is larger than the fŏŏt."
> "The mōōse drank from the cōōl pōōl."
> "He tŏŏk a lŏŏk at the brŏŏk."

In the final analysis, it is the context that helps the child arrive at the correct pronunciation. For convenience in building board- or seat-work exercises, a number of ōō and ŏŏ words are listed below:

ōō				ŏŏ	
bōō	sōōn	mōōn	bōōst	bŏŏk	fŏŏt
cōōl	tōōl	brōōm	lōōp	gŏŏd	tŏŏk
fōōd	bōōt	pōōl	hōōt	stŏŏd	lŏŏk
rōōm	sōōn	lōōse	mōōse	shŏŏk	crŏŏk
tōōth	zōō	rōōt	prōōf	wŏŏd	hŏŏk

There are a few *oo* words which are neither ōō or ŏŏ, such as:

> blood = blŭd;   flood = flŭd
> door = dōr;   floor = flōr

These should be taught as sight words.

DIPHTHONGS

Diphthongs are two adjacent vowels, each of which contributes to the sound heard. The diphthongs discussed here are *ou, ow, oi, oy*. In pronouncing diphthongs, the two vowel sounds are blended as in:

> house   *ow*l   *oi*l   b*oy*

1. The diphthongs *oi* and *oy* have the same sound (boy = boi; toy = toi).

2. The diphthongs *ou* and *ow* have the same sound (plow=plou; bowl=boul).

3. The above vowel combinations are diphthongs only when pronounced as in: h*ou*se, *ow*l, *oi*l, b*oy*.

TEACHING DIPHTHONG SOUNDS

1. Place several words on the board, all of which illustrate **the diphthong** sound of *oi* (column *A*).

A	B
oil	boy
join	toys
noise	joy
point	Roy

2. Pronounce each word for pupils.

3. Have pupils note that these words do not follow the rule: Two vowels together—the first has its long sound, and the second is silent.

4. Point out that each vowel contributes to the sound heard.

5. Place on the board words containing the diphthong *oy* (see column *B*).

6. Point out that *oi* and *oy* sounds are the same.

7. Place on board stimulus words containing diphthong *ou* (see column *A*).

8. Follow steps outlined in Items 2, 3, and 4 above.

A	B
out	down
house	plow
cloud	now
round	clown

9. Place on the board words containing the diphthong *ow*. Pronounce each word.

10. Point out that *ou* and *ow* sounds are the same.

List of diphthong words which might be used in board- or seat-work drill:

cow	owl	mouse	mouth.	boil	boy
how	gown	sound	proud	coin	toy
brown	howl	loud	shout	toil	oyster
tower	brow	couch	found	joint	joy
crown	town	south	count	soil	Troy
powder	fowl	ground	bound	moist	

TEACHING OW AS LONG SOUND OF O

In a number of English words, the *ow* combination has the sound of long ō, and may be taught as follows.

1. The letter combination *ow* has two sounds: the diphthong sound heard in "plow" and the ō heard in "snow."

A	B
cow	low
plow	snow
how	grow
owl	show
town	howl

2. Pronounce the words in column *A*—pupils listening to the sound of *ow*.

3. Pronounce pairs of words: cow, low; pupils listening to contrasting sounds.

4. Pupils pronounce words.

5. Point out that as words are read in context, the proper sound becomes obvious since the children know these words.

HOMONYMS

Homonyms are words that have the same pronunciation but different spellings and meanings. These words involve both structural- and phonic-analysis skills. Some homonyms follow one of the generalizations introduced previously, many do not. For example, the rule, "two vowels together—the first is long, and the second is silent," applies to both words in the following pairs:

meet—meat; see—sea; week—weak

In some instances the above rule applies to one word in a pair, the final *-e* rule to the other word:

road—rode; sail—sale; pain—pane

Some pairs involve silent consonants:

rap—wrap; new—knew; our—hour

Other examples of phonic irregularities:

wait—weight; wood—would; ate—eight; piece—peace

Other homonyms which might be used in board- or seat-work exercises:

beat—beet	maid—made	pair—pare
know—no	so—sew	mail—male
hear—here	hair—hare	steel—steal
there—their	by—buy	waist—waste
sun—son	fair—fare	one—won
whole—hole	dear—deer	some—sum
oh—owe	not—knot	tail—tale

SUMMARY

There is considerable variability in the sound of vowels and vowel combinations in English. This increases the difficulty of teaching or learning vowel sounds. The sequence in which vowel sounds are taught—that is, whether to teach long or short sounds first, or which vowels to teach first—is probably not an issue of great significance. A number of illustrative procedures for teaching are included above. These are meant to be illustrative rather than prescriptive. A number of generalizations covering vowel situations are also discussed above. These include the following:

1. A single vowel in medial position in a word or syllable usually has its short sound (man, bed, fit).

Exceptions:

a) The vowel *o* followed by *ld* usually has its long sound: sōld— cōld; ōld—gōld.

b) The vowel *i* followed by *nd, gh, ld* often has its long sound: fīnd —līght—chīld.

c) The vowel *a* = *aw* when it is followed by *l, ll, w, u*: walk, fall, draw, because.

d) A vowel followed by the letter *r* results in a blended sound which is neither the short nor long sound of the vowel: car, her, for.

e) The spelling *ir* is usually pronounced *ur* (bird = burd) except when followed by a final *e* (fire).

2. When there are two vowels together, the first usually has its long sound, and the second is silent. (This generalization applies most frequently to *ee, oa, ea, ai*: fēe̸d, bōa̸t, bēa̸t, māi̸l.)

3. "In words with two vowels, one of which is final *e*, the *e* is usually silent and the first vowel is usually long." (tāke̸, tūbe̸)

4. "*Ay* at the end of a word has the long sound of *a*." (may, pay, play)

5. "When the only vowel in a word (or accented syllable) comes at the end of the word (or syllable), it usually has its long sound."

6. "When *y* concludes a word of two or more syllables, it has the sound heard in *lucky, badly*." (sometimes taught as short *i*: *luck i;* sometimes as long *e*)

Y functions as a vowel

a) when it concludes a word which has no other vowel

b) when it concludes words of more than one syllable (happy)

c) when it follows another vowel (may).

7. Diphthongs are two adjacent vowels, each of which contributes to the sound heard (h*ou*se, pl*ow*, *oi*l, b*oy*).

8. "The combination *ow* is sometimes pronounced as long *ō*." (snow, show—context provides major clue to pronunciation)

SIGHT-WORD LIST AND INFORMAL PHONICS TEST:

Table 8 is a list of words, most of which are met in primary reading, which illustrate irregular spellings. From the standpoint of spoken language, all words are phonetic. However, the spellings of these words (visual patterns) are such that the more common phonic generalizations learned in beginning reading will not apply.

Table 9 is an informal test of phonic skills consisting of seven brief subtests.

TABLE 8: SIGHT-WORD LIST

(Words with irregular spelling and pronunciation)

above	could	ghost	love	quiet	together
across	couple	give			too
again	cousin	gives	machine	ranger	ton
against	cruel	gloves	many	ready	tongue
aisle	curve	gone	measure	really	touch
already		great	might	right	two
another	dead	guard	mild	rough	
answer	deaf	guess	million		use
any	debt	guest	mind	said	usual
anxious	desire	guide	mischief	says	
	do		minute	science	vein
bear	does	have	move	scissors	very
beautiful	done	head	mother	school	view
beauty	don't	heaven	Mr.	sew	
because	doubt	heart	Mrs.	shoe	was
been	double	heavy		should	wash
behind	dove	here	neighbor	sign	weather
bind	dozen	high	neither	snow	weight
believe			night	soften	were
both	early	idea	none	soldier	what
bough	earn	Indian		some	where
bread	eight	isle	ocean	sometime	who
break	enough	instead	of	someone	whom
bright	eye		office	something	whose
brought	eyes	key	often	son	wild
build		kind	oh	soul	wind

Table 8 (Cont.)

bury	father	knee	once	special	wolf
busy	fence	knew	one	steak	woman
built	field	knife	onion	spread	women
buy	fight	know	only	square	won
	find		other	straight	would
captain	folks	language	ought	sure	wrong
calf	freight	laugh		sword	
caught	friend	laughed	patient		you
chief	front	leather	piece	their	young
child	four	library	pretty	there	your
clothes		light	pull	they	
coming	garage	live	purpose	though	
colt	get	lived	push	thought	
cough	getting	lion	put	to	

TABLE 9: PHONICS-SKILLS TEST

Subtest A (pronunciation)

(Initial and final consonant sounds; short vowel sounds)

dad	self	but	ten	lift
fuss	yell	hog	sand	muff
lamp	him	jug	get	nap
puff	web	miss	pond	kill
rag	gum	pill	rob	cob
van	top	big	held	fond

Subtest B (pronunciation)

(Initial consonant blends; long and short vowel sounds)

bring	split	blue	smoke	scream
throat	clay	club	string	trip
please	twist	float	trade	glass
sky	prize	grass	flag	snail
crop	drill	blow	scene	sweet
spray	free	sled	spoon	stay

Subtest C (pronunciation)

(Consonant digraphs [ch, sh, th, wh, qu, ng, ck]; consonant blends)

quite	thank	check	shrink	crash
church	block	length	queen	shake
shake	quick	shove	choose	think
splash	strong	thing	truck	deck
whale	chose	which	sprung	hung
fresh	wheat	quench	tenth	quack

Table 9 (Cont.)

Subtest D (pronunciation)
(Compound words; inflectional endings; contractions)

keeping	something	it's	bakery	really
pleased	can't	everybody	likes	finding
stops	quickly	lived	someone	helped
I'll	into	calls	he'll	outside
anyone	tallest	you'll	prettiest	loudest
unlock	happily	going	everything	wasn't

Subtest E (syllabication)
(In the blank spaces, write the word in separate syllables.)

candy	can dy	detective	
moment		situation	
locomotive		tiger	
formation		education	
summer		slippery	
tumble		release	

Subtest F (Prefixes, suffixes, and syllabication)
(Pronounce each word; divide each word into syllables [see example].)

dis/con/tent/ment	prehistorical	disloyalty
recaptured	disgraceful	indebtedness
incapable	imperfection	previewing
unhappily	expandable	readjustment
exporter	independently	impassable
removable	rearrangement	submerged

Subtest G
(Sustained-reading passage)

Fred and Frank planned to go on a trip to the pond. Frank liked to swim, but Fred was not a swimmer. He chose to hunt frogs and trap crabs. With a shout, the boys were off on their hike to the lake. At first, they tried to walk in the shade. Then both took off their shirts to get a sun tan.

77

Chapter 4

Syllabication: Prefixes, Suffixes, and Accent

The total word-analysis program includes many related skills. A child learns to profit from a variety of clues such as context, pictures, and phonic analysis. Phonics instruction deals with a number of skills, one of which is syllabication. A syllable is a vowel or a group of letters containing a vowel which form a pronounceable unit. The ability to break words into syllables is a very important word-analysis skill and cuts across both phonic and structural analysis.

Syllabication is an aid in:

1. pronouncing words not instantly recognized as sight words
2. arriving at correct spelling (in phonetic words)
3. breaking words at the end of a line of writing.

Although a number of the more common rules of syllabication are cited and illustrated below, it is not implied that children should memorize such a list of rules. However, familiarity with the principles covered in the various rules is important and desirable.

When the facile reader meets an unknown polysyllabic word, he does not call to mind the rules which might apply. Yet, the responses he makes are undoubtedly related to previous learnings and are conditioned by familiarity with certain principles of syllabication. The ability to pronounce or to approximate the pronunciation of longer unknown words is built on the recognition of both structural and phonetic features of words.

Two major clues to syllabication are prefixes-suffixes, and certain vowel-consonant behavior in written words. Despite the fact that there are numerous exceptions to most generalizations dealing with syllabication, these are still useful to pupils aspiring to become independent readers. With practice, syllabication tends to become an automatic process. There will be considerable agreement among different readers when they pronounce the following nonsense words: pumsaltic, obsebong, besmoray, motsemflo, absolo. (The syllabication patterns arrived at would probably be: pum·sal·tic, ob·se·bong, bes·mo·ray, mot·sem·flo, ab·so·lo.)

RULES FOR BREAKING WORDS INTO SYLLABLES

RULE I: There are as many syllables as there are vowel *sounds*. Syllables are determined by the vowel sounds heard—not by the number of vowels seen.

No. of vowels seen		No. of vowels heard		No. of vowels seen		No. of vowels heard	
1. phonics	2	2	fŏn ĭks	cheese	3	1	chēz
2. write	2	1	rīt	which	1	1	hwĭch
3. release	4	2	rē lēs	precaution	5	3	prē kô shŭn

RULE II: Syllables divide between double consonants—or between two consonants.

hap·pen	can·non	sud·den	ves·sel	vol·ley	com·mand
bas·ket	tar·get	cin·der	har·bor	tim·ber	wig·wam

List of words in which rule holds:

little	sudden	tunnel	after	window	candy
summer	cattle	button	pencil	canvas	basket

daddy	supper	robber	corner	**silver**	master
lesson	dollar	barrel	number	person	center
rabbit	bottom	valley	garden	napkin	silver
funny	letter	rubber	harbor	cargo	wander
carrot	ribbon	follow	picnic	chimney	circus
common	grammar	settle	submit	thunder	husband
suggest	copper	ladder	donkey	object	walrus

RULE III: A single consonant between vowels usually goes with the second vowel.

fa mous	ho tel	di rect	pu pil	ti ger	ce ment
ea ger	wa ter	po lice	spi der	lo cate	va cant

Common words which follow rule:

a round	pi rate	ra dar	be cause	a lone
be gin	fi nal	be fore	pi lot	li bel
pa rade	e lect	re ceive	lo cal	sta tion
mo ment	ba by	di rect	me ter	to day
fro zen	In dian	se vere	sto ry	so lo
ma rine	a bout	de cide	fa tal	si lent

Note: Although this rule is cited extensively in the literature on reading, the exceptions to it are numerous.

Note: Rules I and II above are often combined: Divide *between* two consonants and in *front* of one.

RULE IV: As a general rule, do not divide consonant digraphs (*ch, th,* etc.) and consonant blends.

tea*ch* er	wea*th* er	ma *ch*ine	se *cr*et	a *gr*ee
bro*th* er	prea*ch* er	a*th* lete	coun *tr*y	cel e *br*ate

RULE V: The word endings *-ble, -cle, -dle, -gle, -kle, -ple, -tle, -zle* constitute the final syllable.

mar ble	mus cle	han dle	sin gle	an kle	tem ple
ket tle	puz zle	no ble	pur ple	bat tle	bu gle

Following is a list of words which can be used in building board- or seat-work exercises. Instruct your students to practice on these words so that they can recognize and pronounce each one instantly. Point out how easy it is to learn to spell these words.

no ble	rat tle	sin gle	han dle	tem ple	an kle
mar ble	ket tle	wig gle	mid dle	ma ple	spar kle
sta ble	ti tle	jun gle	pad dle	ap ple	wrin kle
tum ble	bat tle	strug gle	bun dle	sam ple	sprin kle
trou ble	bot tle	gig gle	fid dle	pur ple	crin kle
fa ble	gen tle	bu gle	bri dle	stee ple	tin kle
dou ble	cat tle	ea gle	nee dle	sim ple	puz zle
rum ble	man tle	an gle	sad dle	un cle	fiz zle
peb ble	set tle	shin gle	kin dle	cir cle	muz zle
bub ble	lit tle	strag gle	pud dle	ve hi cle	daz zle

RULE VI: In general, prefixes and suffixes form separate syllables.

re load *ing*	*un* fair	*dis* agree *ment*	*pre* heat *ed*
hope *less*	*trans* port *able*	*un* like *ly*	ex cite *ment*

There are a number of suffixes which appear with high frequency in English words. Instant recognition of these word endings is a considerable help in word analysis. Fortunately, a number are extremely consistent in that they are always *pronounced* the same and always constitute the final syllable. The following list of words ending in *-ment, -tive, -tion, -sion, -ous* may be used in a number of ways to help children *see* and *hear* common phonic elements in words. These words will give:

1. practice in sight-word recognition (Read down the columns as rapidly as possible.)

2. practice in sounding longer words (those not instantly recognized as sight words)

3. practice in breaking words into syllables

4. help in teaching spelling of words (in conjunction with Items 2 and 3 above).

Word list for practice of sight recognition and pronunciation of words ending in *-ment*—always pronounced as in: move *ment*, a part *ment:*

payment	treatment	movement	measurement
statement	pavement	amusement	excitement

enrollment	monument	element	announcement
amazement	punishment	investment	refreshment
basement	equipment	department	agreement
improvement	resentment	management	government
argument	apartment	enjoyment	assignment
moment	advertisement	document	astonishment
settlement	adjustment	amendment	instrument

The word ending *-tion*—always pronounced *shun:*

lotion	motion	education	exception
invention	selection	mention	edition
election	promotion	condition	situation
location	friction	formation	section
direction	construction	subtraction	nation
attraction	vacation	foundation	solution
operation	fraction	position	objection
question	collection	intention	production
addition	population	affection	station

The word ending *-tive*—always pronounced *tiv:*

active	locomotive	objective	relative
positive	destructive	elective	motive
native	adjective	sensitive	attractive
detective	legislative	protective	creative
talkative	attentive	executive	selective

The word ending *-ous* is generally unstressed *ŭs:*

dangerous	curious	enormous	courteous
previous	nervous	poisonous	prosperous
furious	generous	studious	numerous
mysterious	continuous	industrious	tedious

TEACHING PREFIXES AND SUFFIXES AS UNITS

The teaching of prefixes and suffixes involves dealing with a number of word-analysis skills which might be discussed under *structural analysis, phonic analysis,* or *syllabication.* Prefixes and suffixes are structural changes appended to root words. As such, they are also phonic units and, in a majority of cases, constitute syllables.

The first words children learn in reading are root words (look, come, run, talk), but even in grade one, they are systemically introduced to a number of inflectional endings: look*ed,* com*ing,* talk*s,* happ*ily.* As a child successfully progresses in reading, he will meet numerous prefixes and suffixes. Teaching these units must involve both structure and meaning. Generalizations about prefixes and suffixes are discussed below.

1. Prefixes added to words give us new words—often with quite different meanings: clean, *un*clean; read, *re*read; place, *dis*place. Suffixes are word endings which, when added to root words, give us different words. Some of these cause radical changes in meaning (hope, hope*less*) ; others simply give us words which perform different grammatical functions (happy, happily; luck, lucky, luckily).

2. Common endings which begin with a vowel (-er, -est, -ing, -en, -able) are usually sounded as syllables.

3. One-vowel words ending in a single consonant usually double that consonant before adding an ending which begins with a vowel (run— running; stop—stopped; beg—beggar).

This fact may be taught as either structural or phonic analysis. Learning may be facilitated through board-work or seat-work exercises. The above rule may be illustrated as follows:

TABLE 10

	Add endings:		Other endings: -ar, -er, -art
Root	*-ed*	*-ing*	*-ery, -ist, -ary, etc.*
beg	begged	begging	beggar
dim	dimmed	dimming	dimmer
stop	stopped	stopping	stopper
slip	slipped	slipping	slippery
drug	drugged	drugging	druggist
can	canned	canning	cannery
sum	summed	summing	summary
pop	————	————	————
trot	————	————	————
brag	————	————	————
plan	————	————	————
rip	————	————	————
log	————	————	————
slim	————	————	————

Other words which may be used in exercises:

ship, chop, trap, bat, spot, skin, stir, flap, fan, pit, cop, pad, rap, bag, snag, map, pat, hop, hug, fun, top, hot, pop, tag, nap, pet, mop, bet.

Practice Exercise

In columns *A* and *B*, write new words by adding -*ed*, -*ing*.

Make new words by adding one of these endings: -*y*, -*er*, -*en*.

	A	B
	add -*ed*	add -*ing*

Root word

Root word		
pet	_____	_____
skin	_____	_____
step	_____	_____
plan	_____	_____
tap	_____	_____
trim	_____	_____
fit	_____	_____

Root word

Root word	
mud	_____
win	_____
hid	_____
plan	_____
shop	_____
fun	_____
skin	_____
wet	_____

Inflectional endings involve both structural and phonic elements and no effort should be made to separate these elements of word analysis. The objective in teaching these units is to have the child see the structural changes involved and associate the proper language sound with the letter combinations. These sounds are already known by the child, from his language experiences involved in speaking and listening. What is known must now be extended to the printed form of language.

FORMING PLURALS

1. Most plurals are formed by adding *s* to the root word: words, boys, trees, birds, cars, houses, periods, schools, paints, teachers, desks, books, girls, pets.

2. Add *es* to words which end in: s, ss, ch, sh, x.

s	*ss*	*ch*	*sh*	*x*
bus	dress	lunch	dish	fox
busses	dresses	lunches	dishes	foxes

3. When words end with *y*—change the *y* to *i*—then add *es*.

fly—flies; army—armies; penny—pennies

Examples of board- or seat-work exercises follow:

A. When words end in *s, ss, ch, sh, x,* plurals are formed by adding *es.* Write the plural for each of the following words. Note how the plural looks.

box	boxes	kiss	_____	wish	_____
glass	_____	couch	_____	class	_____
bench	_____	inch	_____	flash	_____
peach	_____	splash	_____	brush	_____

Other stimulus words appropriate for this exercise:
branch, pass, witch, fox, speech, brush, guess, inch, loss, watch, ditch, wash, sketch, gas, ax, ranch, mess, tax, bunch, miss, mix

B. When a word ends in *y,* its plural is formed by changing the *y* to *i* and adding *es.* Write the plural for each of the following words:

fly	_____	candy	_____	body	_____
baby	_____	party	_____	lady	_____
puppy	_____	cry	_____	fairy	_____

(cooky, kitty, family, funny, grocery, beauty, buddy, canary, city, dairy, cherry, jelly, factory, enemy, berry, copy, country, dolly, salary, daisy)

C. To form plurals of these words you may add *s, es,* or change final *y* to *i* then add *es.* Write the plural form for each word:

tax	_____	city	_____	dress	_____
tree	_____	match	_____	skirt	_____
pass	_____	copy	_____	dish	_____

Change *y* to *i* before adding a suffix beginning with a vowel.
When a final *y* is the only vowel in the word or in the final syllable— change the *y* to *i* before adding a suffix beginning with a vowel.

Exception: If the suffix begins with *i*, leave the *y*.

Word	*Common endings beginning with a vowel*				*Note*
	-*ed*	-*er*	-*est*	-*ous*:	
busy:	busied				Suffix beginning
fury:				furious	with *i*, do not
dry:	dried	drier	driest		change this *y*.
muddy:	muddied	muddier	muddiest		crying
happy:		happier	happiest		drying
glory:				glorious	frying
carry:	carried	carrier			flying
					copying
					carrying

Drop final *e* before adding a suffix beginning with a vowel.

large + er = larger; + est = largest.
hate + ing = hating; + ed = hated.
wide + er = wider; + est = widest.

COMPOUND WORDS

A large number of English words are formed by combining two words. While a relatively small number of compounds are encountered in beginning reading, beyond this stage more and more of these words are met. Recognition of compound words is achieved through every type of word-analysis skill (structural analysis, phonic analysis, and context examination). When teaching compound words, each of these aids should be employed. It should be noted particularly that sight-word drill, and structural-phonic analysis go hand in hand. The following points should be kept in mind:

1. Compound words are part of the child's speaking and meaning vocabulary before he learns them as sight-recognition units.

2. The meaning of compound words is derived from combining two words.

3. The pronunciation of the compound word remains the same as the two combining forms (except for accent or stress).

4. With the above points in mind, a child will not be likely to develop a set to "find little words in big words." His ear and mind will reject:

> "So me time" for sometime,
> "go at me at" for goat meat,
> "he posted a not ice on the camp us."

Procedures for teaching compound words will vary with the instruction level. A few techniques are illustrated:

A	B
in	to
any	one
some	thing
door	way

1. Place words in columns *A* and *B* on board.

2. "Here are some words we have learned as sight words—let's read these words together."

3. "Sometimes we combine two words to make a new word—we call these words compound words." (Combine words in *A* and *B*; ask children to pronounce each word. Ask various children to use the compound word in a sentence.)

in to—into	some thing—something
any one—anyone	door way—doorway

4. Seat-work exercises may be developed to parallel above.

A. "See the words under *A* and *B*—write them together to form a new word."

A	B	C
up	on	upon
some	time	_____
him	self	_____
mail	box	_____
after	noon	_____
hat	box	_____

B. "Each word in Column 1 can be placed with a word in Column 2 to make a new word (or compound word). The first one is done for you."

1	2	3
*rain	plane	*raincoat
sail	out	_____
air	*coat	_____
every	body	_____
with	boat	_____

C. "In your own words, write a definition for each of the compound words below."

1. beeswax: "_____"
2. rowboat: "_____"
3. drawbridge: "_____"
4. spellbound: "_____"
5. sharpshooter: "_____"

D. One of the words at the right will combine with each of   *bath*
the words in the columns below. Write a compound word in each   *door*
blank.   *board*
   boat

_____way	sail_____	_____room	out_____
_____man	row_____	_____tub	over_____
_____step	steam_____	_____mat	score_____
_____stop	motor_____	_____house	chess_____

Compound words for board- or seat-work exercises:

Primary level   *Intermediate level*

anyway	anyone	upset	salesman	downpour	blacksmith
something	evergreen	without	lifetime	fingertip	notebook
whenever	afternoon	birthday	lighthouse	shortstop	highpower
himself	airport	basketball	countryside	houseboat	blowout
snowman	sandbox	swordfish	peppermint	floodlight	taxpayer
windshield	herself	clubhouse	grasshopper	otherwise	overgrown
toothbrush	railroad	upstairs	flagpole	eyeball	riverbank
motorcycle	bookcase	barefoot	peacetime	pigtail	undersize
broadcast	horseshoe	typewriter	lifejacket	classmate	toothache
aircraft	lighthouse	anthill	broadcast	slowpoke	marksman

FINDING LITTLE WORDS IN BIG WORDS

In the past, considerable confusion has arisen over this particular practice. It was once quite common, in materials prepared for teachers, to suggest that children be taught to "look for little words in big words." The theory was that after a child has learned to recognize smaller words, it would be useful to him as a reader if he would "see" these smaller units when they were part of larger words. This, it was alleged, would help him solve or pronounce the larger words.

This practice, of course, has only very limited utility or justification. It is justifiable when dealing with compound words or known root words to which have been added prefixes or suffixes. However, in general, the habit of seeing little words in big words will actually interfere with sounding out words in a great number of instances. This is true even in beginning reading; but once a child is beyond this stage, this practice has practically no justification whatsoever.

To illustrate, let us look at some of the more common "little words." In each of the following, if the child sees and pronounces the little word, he cannot arrive at the pronunciation of the word under attack.

at:	bo at	b at h	pl at e	o at	at e	at omic
	r at e	pot at o	co at	at hlete	he at	
as:	bo as t	ple as e	As ia	co as t	as hore	
on:	on e	t on e	d on e	h on ey	st on e	
he:	he at	he lp	c he st	bat he	t he y	w he at
me:	me at	a me n	ca me	sa me	a me nd	

Hundreds of other examples could be added using the above and other little words such as: *in, an, it, am, if, us, is, to, up, go, no, lid, are, or,* etc. Little words (or their spellings) occur frequently in larger polysyllabic words, but the pronounceable autonomy of the little words in big words is often lost. Therefore teaching children to "look for little words in big words" has little justification from the standpoint of phonic or structural analysis.

ACCENT

Each syllable in polysyllabic words is not spoken with the same force or stress. These variations in stress are called "accent.." The syllable which receives the most stress is said to have the *primary* accent (car′ pen ter). Other syllables in a given word may have a secondary (lesser) accent, or syllables may be unaccented (in′ vi ta′ tion).

Teaching *accent* is usually reserved for the later stages of word analysis. The majority of words met in beginning reading consist of one or two syllables. Longer words met are those which a child has probably heard or spoken hundreds of times (yesterday, grandmother, afternoon, tomorrow, telephone).

Accent is important in using a dictionary when the objective is to determine the pronunciation of a word. It is important in reading when a child meets a word he does not know on sight but has heard and whose meaning he knows. For instance, if a child has heard or used the word "celebration" or "appendicitis," but does not recognize the printed symbols, he may distort its pronunciation through improper syllabication: ce le bra tion, ce leb ra tion; or improper accent: ap′ pen *di′* ci tis.

Skills to be taught include:

1. How to read primary- and secondary-accent marks in the dictionary
2. The habit of "trying" different soundings if the first attempt does not result in a known word.
3. The use of "clues" or rules of accent in attempting the pronunciation of words. Some of these follow:

   a) In compound words, the primary accent usually falls on (or within) the first word (sail′ boat; wolf′ hound; fish′ er man; door′ way; police′ man).

   b) In two-syllable words containing a double consonant, the accent usually falls on the first syllable (cop′ per; mil′lion; pret′ ty; val′ ley; sud′ den).

   c) When *ck* ends a syllable, that syllable is usually accented (chick′ en; rock′ et; pack′ age; nick′ el; mack′ er el).

   d) Syllables comprised of a consonant plus *le* are usually not accented (ble, cle, dle, gle, ple, tle). Many of the instances covered by the above rules might be summarized under one inclusive generalization:

In two-syllable root words, the accent usually falls on the first syllable —except when the second syllable contains two vowels.

   (Exceptions occur in a number of words in which the last syllable contains two vowels—particularly if one is final *e*: be lieve′; pa rade′; sur prise′; sus tain′; ma chine′; sup pose′.)

e) Prefixes and suffixes, as a rule, are not accented (lone′ ly; un hap′ pi ly; re fresh′ ment; dis re spect′ ful; re tract′ a ble).

f) Two-syllable words ending with *y* are usually accented on the first syllable (cit′ y; ear′ ly; ba′ by; can′ dy; sto′ ry; par′ ty; fun′ ny; mer′ ry; tru′ ly).

g) Adding suffixes to some longer words may cause a shift in the primary accent. Words in column *A* have the primary accent on the first or second syllables, but in column *B* (derived forms) the accent has shifted.

A	B
u′ ni verse	u ni ver′ sal
mi′ cro scope	mi cro scop′ ic
vac′ ci nate	vac ci na′ tion
ac′ ci dent	ac ci den′ tal
con firm′	con fir ma′ tion

Generalization:

In many longer words the primary accent falls on the syllable before the suffix.

(Exception: In most cases the primary accent falls two syllables before suffix *-ate*: ag′ gra vate; dom′ i nate; ed′ u cate; hes′ i tate; med′ i tate; op′ er ate.)

h) Homographs—and accent shift (homo = same; graph = to write: homograph = same writing).

Homographs are words with identical spellings, different meanings, and, in some cases, different pronunciations. The sentences below contain homographs. It will be noted that usage or context determines the pronunciation. (Changes may take place in accent or in both accent and syllabication.)

present = pre/sent′, pres′/ent; content = con/tent′, con′/tent

1. The mayor was *present* to *present* the awards.
2. The editor was not *content* with the *content* of the article.
3. Always be careful to *address* the letter to the correct *address*.

The following words may be used in teaching exercises:

lead—lead	live—live	object—object
close—close	excuse—excuse	read—read
protest—protest	wind—wind	contract—contract

perfect—perfect	subject—subject	combine—combine
convict—convict	annex—annex	produce—produce
permit—permit	rebel—rebel	conduct—conduct

USE OF THE DICTIONARY—AS A WORD-ATTACK SKILL

As the child becomes an independent reader, he is likely to meet a number of words which

1. he does not know or use in his speaking vocabulary
2. cannot be easily solved by applying phonic generalizations.

Since the dictionary is a source for the pronunciation of words, certain dictionary skills are, in effect, word-analysis skills. Effective use of the dictionary involves learning the speech equivalents of visual symbols including primary- and secondary-accent marks; diacritical marks such as the macron (‾) (make = māk); the breve (˘) (ăt); the schwa (ə) (ten dər); etc.

Different dictionaries and glossaries found in textbooks may use a variety of symbols, or phonetic spellings, all of which will have to be mastered. For example:

> technique: tek nēk; tĕk nēk; tek neek
> temperament: tem′ pər ə mənt; tĕm pĕr á ment

(For a discussion of the schwa sound, see page 59.)

The *pronunciation key* of the dictionary or dictionaries used should be taught. The dictionary will be of little value in arriving at the correct pronunciation of words if these various symbols are not mastered.

CONCLUSION

Whether or not phonic analysis should be taught as part of the reading program is not an issue. Children need this important ability in order to become independent readers. However, in recent years, the matter of phonics instruction has become a major educational issue in the teaching of reading. This issue developed in a round-about way, in that critics of American reading instruction have planted the idea that present day methodology is opposed to teaching phonics and that materials and instruction make no provision for teaching phonic analysis skills.

While both of these premises are false, they are the basis for the debate over "phonetic method *vs* the sight-word method." Confusion has resulted because critics, laymen, and teachers are, by the very nature of this debate, forced to take a polar position on phonics instruction. As a result, we have tended to lose sight of *the purpose of phonics instruction as it relates to learning to read*. The "either/or" discussion has covered up and ignored some important educational implications of phonics instruction.

One of the purposes of this book is to identify and explore a number of such educational issues. The following is a brief summary of the points discussed previously:

1. The purpose of phonics instruction, as it relates to reading, is to provide the child with the skill for pronouncing or approximating the pronunciation, of words not known as sight words.

2. The term, *word-analysis skills*, embraces *all* ways in which a child might "solve" a word which he does not recognize.

3. Phonics is but one important part of this total word analysis program. Children solve words by means of unique features ("tt", "ll", "oo", "y") ; pictures; structural analysis; context; phonic analysis—as well as utilizing these methods in combination.

4. Children can be taught overreliance on sounding out words. Overreliance on any one of the above approaches is not efficient. The child who can "sound" all words and who does sound out all words is an inefficient reader.

5. Early reading instruction should not provide a "set" for sounding each word.

6. Beginning reading instruction should foster a set that "reading is a meaning-making process." In initial reading instruction, one teaches some words as wholes before teaching sounds of letters in words. Then, as quickly as possible, words should be mastered as sight-recognition vocabulary.

7. When analysis is begun,

   a) words already learned are used as phonic models,

   b) consonants are taught first because their sounds are more consistent than vowel sounds,

   c) words are attacked from left-to-right (more than 80% of words begin with consonants), and *d*) children are taught to use all methods of word analysis (structural, context, phonics).

8. A good phonics program provides for differentiated instruction. The right combination of phonics instruction for "Child A" may be inadequate for "Child B" and excessive for "Child C." For any given child, the right combination of drill on analysis is the *minimum* he needs to arrive at the pronunciation of words whose meanings he presently knows.

A second objective of this material is to present a brief outline of practices which might be used in teaching phonic analysis. The suggestions were intended to be illustrative rather than prescriptive. Some of the principles outlined include:

1. The basis for all instruction in phonics is the ability to discriminate between speech sounds and the ability to visually discriminate between printed letters.

2. Having the child memorize rules does not assure that he can, or will, apply these in reading situations.

3. All phonic principles necessary for a child to become an independent reader should be taught.

4. It is not necessary to teach phonic generalizations which have very limited application. The few words covered by such generalizations should be taught as sight words.

5. Teachers at various grade levels should be familiar with the entire phonics program because of the variability of children's needs in a given classroom.

BIBLIOGRAPHY

BIBLIOGRAPHY

(A limited number of sources which contain suggestions for teaching phonics)

Agnew, Donald C. *Effect of Varied Amounts of Phonetic Training on Primary Reading.* Durham, N.C.: Duke University Press, 1939.

Bloomfield, Leonard and Clarence L. Barnhart. *Let's Read—A Linguistic Approach.* Detroit: Wayne State University Press, 1961.

Bond, Guy L. and Eva Bond Wagner. *Teaching the Child to Read.* (3rd ed.). New York: Macmillan Co., 1960.

Burrows, Alvina Trent. *What About Phonics.* Bulletin No. 75. Washington, Association for Childhood Education, 1951.

Dawson, Mildred A. and Henry A. Bamman. *Fundamentals of Basic Reading Instruction.* (chap. 6). New York: Longmans, Green & Co., Inc., 1959.

Dechant, Emerald V. *Improving the Teaching of Reading.* (chaps. 10-11) Englewood Cliffs, N.J.: Prentice-Hall, Inc., 1964.

Dolch, William E. *The Teaching of Sounding.* Champaign, Ill.: Garrard Publishing Co., 1951.

Durkin, Dolores. *Phonics and the Teaching of Reading.* (Bureau of Publications, No. 22) New York: Teachers College, Columbia University, 1962.

Durrell, Donald D. *Improving Reading Instruction.* (chaps. 11-12) Yonkers-on-Hudson: World Book Co., 1956.

Education. Vol. LXXV, 1955. (The entire issue is devoted to phonics.)

Gray, Lillian. *Teaching Children to Read.* (3rd ed.) New York: The Ronald Press Company, 1963.

Gray, William S. *On Their Own In Reading.* (Rev. ed.) Chicago: Scott, Foresman & Company, 1960.

Heilman, Arthur W. *Principles and Practices of Teaching Reading.* (chap. 7) Columbus, Ohio: Charles E. Merrill Books, Inc., 1961.

Herr, Selma E. *Phonics Handbook for Teachers.* Los Angeles: E.R.A. Publishers, Inc., 1961.

Hildreth, Gertrude. "The Role of Pronouncing and Sounding in Learning to Read," *Elementary School Journal,* LV (November 1954), 141-47.

Learning to Read. Princeton, N.J.: Educational Testing Service, 1962. (A report of a conference of reading experts.)

McKee, Paul. *The Teaching of Reading in the Elementary School.* (chaps. 8-11) Boston: Houghton Mifflin Company, 1948.

"Phonics in Reading Instruction," *Reading Teacher.* Vol. IX, December 1955.

Russell, David H. *Children Learn to Read.* (chap. 10) Boston: Ginn & Company, 1961.

INDEX

INDEX